Actress to Actress

Oct.   1986

Best wishes

Rita Gam

Actress to Actress

RITA GAM

NICK LYONS BOOKS • NEW YORK

The chapter on Grace Kelly appeared, in somewhat different form, in *McCall's* magazine.

Typeset by Fisher Composition, Inc.

Printed in the United States of America

10 9 8 7 6 5 4 3 2 1

Library of Congress Cataloging-in-Publication Data

Gam, Rita.
   Actress to actress.

   Includes index.
   1. Actresses—Biography. I. Title.
PN2205.G3   1986   792′.028′0922 [B]   86–18572
ISBN 0–941130–23–1

Special thanks to M-G-M, 20th Century-Fox, Warner Bros., Universal Pictures, United Artists, Columbia Pictures, and Paramount Pictures for use of their publicity pictures in this book. Special thanks, too, to Judith Weiss, who with patience typed the transcripts and then my text for *Actress to Actress*.

Contents

PREFACE *by Robert Whitehead* · *vii*

INTRODUCTION · *1*

Part One · STARS OF FILM · 15

Grace Kelly · *17*
Jeanne Moreau · *27*
Susannah York · *35*
Shelley Winters · *43*
The Mavericks—Jane Fonda, Jessica Lange,
Vanessa Redgrave, Meryl Streep · *52*

Part Two · THEATRE VOICES · 63

Julie Harris · *65*
Glenda Jackson · *77*
Maureen Stapleton · *86*
Zoe Caldwell · *94*
Actors Studio Originals—Viveca Lindfors and
Geraldine Page · *103*
Joanne Woodward · *113*

Part Three · THE CLASSICAL TEMPER · 121

Wendy Hiller · 123
Constance Cummings · 134
Eva Le Gallienne · 142
Jessica Tandy · 150
Dame Judith Anderson · 159

Part Four · ASCENDING STARS · 169

Julie Walters · 171
The Stars of India · 176
Diane Venora and Elizabeth McGovern · 184

AFTERWORD · 195

Preface

The first time I met Rita Gam, she was sitting on a piano stool in Stella Adler's apartment. She must have been no more than twenty. She was very beautiful and very young and she had soft very large eyes that possessed a questioning eagerness. Whenever the theatre was discussed, which was practically all evening, she responded with a quiet, modest, immense awe, and with respect and idealism. I thought to myself that she didn't need to be so intense in her feeling, because looking as delicious as she did, she was bound to have an adventurous life in any case.

The next thing I knew Rita was becoming a movie star—playing rather exotic temptress-type ladies and other leading parts (which she describes in this book) but I didn't meet her again for about fifteen years. Then it was in my office—she sat on the other side of my desk; I was busy trying to cast an acting company in the early days of Lincoln Center. Rita was anxious to join the company. There was the same girl that sat on that piano stool, the same beauty, the same eyes, the same awe, respect and almost longing for the theatre. Again I thought, in a male chauvinist way, Why is she possessed by this need when she already has so many attributes? Rita in her book both asks and answers that question with charming innocence; she writes, "What is the connection between beauty, which one has little to do with, and the craft of acting?" "What has a million dollars' worth of publicity to do with acting?"

The years passed, even the decades, while Rita and I became

friends. She worked a good deal in the theatre playing many parts (which she touches on in the book), but only occasionally did she find the real satisfaction she was seeking—which, of course, is what happens to most of us.

Now when I read *Actress to Actress,* Rita had by this time acquired a great deal of experience and has known or worked with all the actresses she has chosen to write about. There inside each biography is the warmth, the respect, even the longing—and there in these pages is the girl on the piano stool.

Nobody gets hurt in this book—it is never a gossip column. It is Rita seeking to find an answer to a question that was always in her: "What is it that makes an acting performance suddenly and very occasionally a thing of beauty?"

Her search is filled with questions and answers that are continually provocative—and she writes about these talented actresses with generosity and admiration. *Actress to Actress* is, finally, mighty attractive.

ROBERT WHITEHEAD
May 1986

For my children
KATE AND MICHAEL GUINZBURG

Introduction

W hat makes one actress want to write a book about other actresses?

I was in the middle of writing my autobiography and had begun to look closely at several actresses who were my role models and friends. The process was fascinating. I felt that I could understand myself better if I understood them—that our worlds were intertwined. And just then something happened that both devastated me and brought certain fuzzy notions into painful focus. A longtime friend—also an actress, Grace Kelly—died after a tragic accident. We had roomed together in Hollywood and remained close friends long after she became Princess Grace of Monaco. She turned her back on acting, but never turned off her love for it. I wanted suddenly to write about her—and *for* her.

So I put away my narcissistic odyssey and began to wander the world, to interview interesting and great actresses on several continents for *Actress to Actress*.

I had always been fascinated by other practitioners of the craft. As a curious twelve-year-old I tried on Loretta Young's smile in my bathroom mirror, attempting to capture that wise, witty, and serene face. After thrilling to a Saturday matinee of Tennessee Williams's *The Glass Menagerie*, I attempted to recreate Laurette Taylor's light-filled levitation by sweeping across our living room on Riverside Drive. As I pondered the mystery of her floating movements, I was inspired to ask my mother for my first drama lessons.

Perhaps others will be inspired by my glimpse into the lives of these great actresses—and certainly those who had admired them on stage and film will enjoy knowing about their personal idiosyncrasies.

Grace Kelly. Surely, I would write about her—but about whom else? I confess that my choices are emotional and *very* personal. I worked with some and admired others from afar. Dame Wendy Hiller, Glenda Jackson, Susannah York, Maureen Stapleton, Eva Le Gallienne, Shelley Winters, Jeanne Moreau, Meryl Streep, Jessica Lange, and a host of others, young and old, are here—and I will explore why their very names conjure up such vivid memories for me, such magic. And what the person is really like behind the persona.

I regret not having in the book Katharine Hepburn, who has that uncanny gift for piercing to the heart of truth, or Marlene Dietrich, who for my first premier, *Saadia,* gave me her velvet suit with the black fox. She dispensed homey advice during a period of marital strife with my first husband, Sidney Lumet, and shared her knowledge about acting with me. "Always keep your voice in the low register for films," she said, topping her generosity off with a silver and blue angel for my Christmas tree.

Nor are those wonderful gypsies Gretchen Wyler or Chita Rivera or Shirley MacLaine in the book, but their magic will remain undimmed as long as there is a superhigh kick. I regret their not appearing here as I regret not having noted some words of theatrical wisdom from Françoise Rosay, the great French actress, or the words of magical Dame Peggy Ashcroft. And Goldie Hawn . . .

All the chapters in the book have been written under different circumstances and I didn't adhere to any formal principle when I wrote them. It was an adventure to go around the world to talk to the stars of India, who are as varied as the stars in the heavens. But I was able to recognize the similarities between them and the actresses from America, England, and France. I wanted to talk to Zoe Caldwell, with whom I have had a deep friendship stemming from the days we shared a dressing room in a repertory company in the frozen Middle West, but it was difficult to talk about acting then since we were used to indulging ourselves in personal confidences and always ended up in giggles.

I have known Joanne Woodward for thirty years, and just re-

Viveca Lindfors, Eva Le Gallienne, Judith Anderson, and Rita Gam in CBS–TV's Bridge of San Luis Rey *(1957), written by Thornton Wilder. Courtesy of David Susskind.*

cently had the experience of working with her every day for two months. I recorded that with the joy of new discovery.

I had watched Jessica Lange and Meryl Streep and Vanessa Redgrave from a distance, but I wanted to examine my special feelings of admiration I have about them. Having worked with Eva Le Gallienne as well as with Dame Judith Anderson, I felt they had to be here, so I drove through a blinding Southern California thunderstorm with actress friend Diana Douglas at the wheel to talk to Dame Judith in Santa Barbara, and I spoke on the phone with Eva Le Gallienne in Connecticut.

Grace Kelly and Rita Gam at Gam's engagement party (1956). From the personal collection of Rita Gam.

I tried quite hard to reach and interview Melina Mercouri, now the minister of culture in Greece—once Melina of the uninhibited smile, known for flickering moods, humorous wisdom, and *Never on Sunday*. After spending several days in a frustrating maze of international telephone calls to Athens, I was finally rewarded by someone saying "Hello" in a voice ranging from pianissimo to fortissimo. In the notes of a spoiled child, a sexy woman, and an army general, she said, "Today is May Day; elections are coming up." When I asked to whom I was talking the voice growled, "Angelica—call tomorrow—today *also* is Sunday."

The telephone slammed down, bringing our cryptic conversation to an abrupt stop. I had the distinct impression that I was talking to Melina herself. But the telephone lines were down on Monday and I never got through again. Was it Angelica or really Melina? I'll never know. . . .

I have tried to be representative without being encyclopedic; I have tried following my interests and affections without becoming solipsistic. Mostly, I want to find the special qualities that are found in all actresses—qualities that are always discretely different but seem to overlap.

I want to capture the essence and the magic, but also talk about the craft of acting. Many of my queries were about craft—a craft as exacting as tightrope-walking and perhaps as dangerous, behind which the human spirit shines. I wanted—God, how I wanted—to understand actresses, these mythical creatures, these sisters of mine.

II

The profound fact of an actress's life is that she "acts" on stage, in films, and sometimes in life. Many of us find our identity through the parts we play. We feel whole when we have that second person to portray at night. What is it that drives us? Why are we "on" even in life? Obsession?

In a profession as demanding of dedication as is the case with novitiate nuns, I interviewed the actresses to discover how, where, when, and why we dreamed ourselves into existence. Along with intense interest in the technique and craft of acting, I confess to a reporter's insatiable curiosity about the different paths other actresses' careers have taken. My own career took an unexpected turn when I went to Hollywood for the first time to do a small part in *The Thief*.

A wardrobe woman at United Artists insisted that I wear four pairs of falsies inside my striped T-shirt, creating not only my character in the film but also the worldwide image—"Silent and Sexy," as *Life* said in its cover story on me—a tag that made me famous. But was that acting?

Every once in a while something magical happens between a face and a movie camera—a magic that may consist in little more than taking charisma or beauty and blowing it up forty times larger than life. Many actresses in this book have suffered or enjoyed the same fate. A big advertising budget has made some of them more famous than others.

Because of my dark hair and high cheekbones, I was cast in "ethnic" parts. I was the Mohawk squaw, the Berber princess, the seductive "dark" love interest in costume films, the speck of sex in the spectacle. I became a member of the peripatetic film repertory company of Americans and Britons who were kept buzzing around the world to swagger and pose in the crowded, exotic dense epics so loved in the fifties.

I played Herod's wife in *King of Kings* but lost the part of Moses' wife in *The Ten Commandments* to Yvonne DeCarlo because of my combination of agnosticism and honesty. When Cecil B. DeMille interviewed me for the part, he asked if I believed in God, and a little voice inside me—I shall never know why—counseled me to tell the truth. "Remember that you went to Ethical Culture," the little voice said, and I looked at DeMille and said, distinctly, "No!" Now I always watch *The Ten Commandments* on television with the sinking sense that I might well have been Mrs. Moses.

In order to take advantage of "blocked funds" scattered all over the world, MGM turned *Saadia,* which would ordinarily have been a sand-and-tits epic shot in California, into a tits-and-sand epic shot in Morocco.

There were some spectacular outdoor scenes in *Saadia,* but the ones engraved on my mind were shot in a dank smelly cave. I had to stab to death my French co-star, Michel Simon. I kept missing him. We kept reshooting the scene. For three days I stalked and stabbed at Michel Simon's padded stomach until he slipped just right onto the point of my jewel-encrusted dagger, staggering forward and falling onto a pile of cushions, eyes open and staring up at me. In perfect English he said, "You kill me hard."

In another scene in that awful cave, I had to fend off the lesbian advances of the wicked witch Fatima. "I won't go back to Ananoot," was the line I had to say. It took twenty-seven takes until the director was satisfied that I was projecting genuine horror and disgust. I finally repelled the clawing woman, holding my breath against the stench of that cave, as I said ever more desperately, "I won't go back to Ananoot." Was that acting?

After having starred in several of these adventure films made here and there and around the world, I wanted to "grow" as an actress, in the pure sense of the word, and I began studying The Method at the Actors Studio.

I was naïve, frightened, and very impressed by Lee Strasberg's scholarly articulation. The world of Stanislavsky has to be understood to be conquered, but I was wary of "sense memory" and "effective memory" and the emotions that were supposed to come alive with the use of sensory perception.

Having just come through a period of painful emotionalism in my private life, I was preparing for the part of Cathie in Tennessee Williams's *Suddenly, Last Summer* and I was afraid to tap into my own recent hysteria for fear of a relapse. But, reading the play under the careful watchful eye of teacher Paula Strasberg, I let out all the stops. I was everything in the reading that Cathie had to be, distraught, fragmented, frightened, mad.

I felt that I could not allow myself to do that on stage every night because my own nervous system wasn't up to it. And when Paula looked at me with a steadying gaze and said softly, "How do you feel now after our read through?" I said, "Fine." She replied, "Well, then. . . ?"

Every night before I played Cathie, while standing in the cavernous wings of the South American theatres, I would lean against a wall and imagine I was on Long Island with the noon breeze blowing in from off the ocean and wetting my shoulder with salt water. That brought back a moment of great loss in my life and I went on to act the hell out of the Williams heroine for real. Paula was right; after every performance I felt just fine, and very hungry.

For real? As opposed to acting. And yet what could be more real than acting? I know it sounds like a riddle, but think about it for a minute. What could be more real than makeup under your fingernails, the time spent upon the stage, acting and rehearsing? Is there any more real sound than your agent telling you, "You didn't get the part because you're too old"? What to do? Get a new agent!

Shelley Winters and Rita Gam at an Actor's Studio benefit. From the personal collection of Rita Gam.

And for a nice slice of reality, it's hard to beat being dragged through the mud by your leading man, for twelve takes.

Actress. Say it enough times over and it becomes a nonsense word. Keep on saying it and it turns into a kind of mantra, evoking images of—what?

We are forever dependent on the fickle whims of fashion, on the winds of change. We are at the mercy of the long wait. It is a profession that uses only when it needs. A common dilemma, the "right play," the "right part," the "right review": all things that control us and our theatrical reality. In effect, we are dependent on everything and everyone. A great actress can exist, like a rare gem in Tiffany's window, wasted and unused behind cold glass, or she can be bought and appreciated.

With wonder and admiration I have watched other actresses work. One and all we have had to battle from childhood to old age to achieve perfection. Not from the same traditions, we all have invented new ways to make words fresh. There are similarities in training and background that frequently show. Childhood was a time of expansion; imaginations grew from whatever was around us. All actresses possess that extra degree of energy, that electricity, that magic, that makes them different from other people.

For many of us creative vitality started with our desire to improve the world of our childhood. With that we transmute the lead of mundane existence into artistic gold. Many have had a sense of predestination, a desire to escape from poverty or the boredom of a humdrum existence. And always there is the refusal to be engulfed by the commonplace.

My own experiences as a child could have been those of Julie Harris, or Dame Judith Anderson, or Glenda Jackson, or even of the actresses of India. We all dreamed the same dream at the age of twelve.

Sir Tyrone Guthrie, a director who has affected many creative lives, worked with at least five of the actresses in this book. Dr. Guthrie, as he was called, was one of the greatest directors in the world. Originally from Ireland, he helped to create the Old Vic in London with Laurence Olivier and Sir John Gielgud, and the Stratford Theatre in Canada. Like Johnny Appleseed, he planted theatres wherever he went, from Iceland to Israel.

The first time I became aware of him was on January 20, 1963, when I walked into the still incompleted Guthrie Theatre in Minneapolis. Despite the sub-zero temperature outside, I had a warm feeling inside; I knew instinctively that I had signed up to act with one of the best theatres in the world and to work with a director of magnitude.

I was shyly staring down at the floor when I saw in front of me a very large pair of tennis shoes. I looked up slowly to see a six-foot-five giant, Sir Tyrone Guthrie. He was shaking my hand and gazing over my shoulder at his wife, Lady Judith, who looked remarkably like his twin. Two eagles, they had total, almost super-human, communication.

"Rather a good sort, you know, but terribly nervous, don't you think." He was talking about *me*. At that point someone came over to him and gushed: "Sir Tyrone, you are an absolute genius." He whirled around like a big bear and growled, "Fucky-poo, fucky-poo." Most likely, he was saying "Fucking fool," because Lady Judith, nodding in agreement, said, "He certainly is." I knew then that my time spent with him would be different from anything I had ever known.

Sir Tyrone Guthrie once said, "The theatre is a powerful sexual stimulant, but when its power is not misused it is a powerful awakener of other ideas." All the actresses in the book, regardless of their age, have that special sexual projection that makes the world go round.

On the first day of rehearsal for Chekhov's *Three Sisters,* I launched with gusto into the reading of Masha. The passionate, foolish, lyrical Masha was the part I had really come to Minnesota to play. Chekhov, who had written it for his mistress-wife Olga Knipper, said, "I have written you an actress's dream-part of a lifetime."

Indeed it was. It was Dr. Guthrie's favorite role for an actress, and mine, too. Perhaps I read it with a smidge too much fervor. When the reading was over and I was wiping my stage tears away, Guthrie said, "Well done, all of you, Jessie, Zoe, Hume. And you, Rita," he continued, "no more of that movie-queen sentiment." I burst into tears. "Stop blubbering, Miss Gam, or you can leave the company. Movie queen Gam," he continued sarcastically, "don't wave your hands around like a surburban housewife." I continued weeping hysterically. He pierced me with his sharp blue eyes and I suddenly stopped crying. "I'll stop blubbering," I said, "if you stop calling me a movie queen. Call me Rita and I'll call you Tony." We shook hands on it.

Zoe Caldwell making up at the Tyrone Guthrie Theatre in St. Paul, Minnesota. From the personal collection of Zoe Caldwell.

When rehearsal was over I went to the dressing room that I shared with Zoe Caldwell and crumpled into my chair in a flood of tears. Zoe blew into the room with an institutional "Darling," sat down at her half of the makeup table and began carefully to clean the tops of her makeup jars. She ignored me. Looking at her in the mirror, I said, "I need a friend. Will you be it?" Zoe paused a full sixty seconds and looking back at my mirror image said, "Yes." We have remained close friends ever since.

At the end of the season Tony Guthrie came into our dressing room and asked, "Well, what have you two girls learned from one another?" I bubbled, "Well, I learned how to curse." And Zoe replied in her buckwheat Australian voice, "I learned how to cry."

Many years later, when I played the actress Madame Arkadina in Chekhov's *Sea Gull,* I patterned myself on Zoe. When Zoe played her Madame Arkadina for the BBC in London, she told me she researched the part in the Lincoln Center Library and came across my *New York Times* review and patterned her Madame Arkadina on me. We had come full circle.

I can picture big Tony—magician, bully, schoolmaster, looking down from the ultimate rep, padding around in his tennis shoes, and saying, "Don't complain, don't explain, and for Heaven's sake don't apologize." It is the life lesson we all learned from him.

In some ways this book has been difficult to define because actresses are indefinable.

That's just the point! The actress is indefinable because she must of necessity be *undefined*. She is the blank page of Shakespeare, Saroyan, Molière. She is the tabula rasa, terrifying with its implication of infinite possibility. It is the great actress who conceals her mysteries. Age can be a merciless doodler on the page, or a careful scribe encoding even deeper secrets, and an actress's term of service can be abruptly curtailed when the page is full.

III

Some of the actresses in this book, like Grace Kelly, were old friends; others, like Dame Wendy Hiller, were forbidding, remote figures. Sometimes, when I called on them, my courage seemed about to desert me. When I suddenly had an image of being thrown out into the street, pencils flying, when it all seemed as if it might fall apart—I just took a deep breath and reassured myself of one, undeniable fact: I am an actress, as they are actresses; we share a bond that reaches back to Bernhardt and beyond. I charged forth.

Several actresses and many cities later, I returned from my odyssey with mountains of notes to be sorted, miles of tapes to be transcribed, and some satisfying insights.

I had hoped there might be some great discovery, some common denominator to be found. At first I thought not, but perhaps there was. I saw in all of us the common thread of having a strong mother, and one most often supportive. All of us were highly intelligent and curious, and I *did* begin to observe a curious trait shared to a degree by all, especially by those of a certain age. In fact, it seemed that the older that actresses get, the more they exhibit this mysterious phenomenon.

I am talking about the *light*.

I first really noticed it while talking with Dame Wendy when she described her meeting with George Bernard Shaw. I was particularly taken when she said he was surrounded by a blue light, and I remember doing a mental double take and thinking, but my dear, *you* are positively bursting with light!

It seems to come from inside, as if all those years of taking in the light, being bathed in it, had resulted in the light's being somehow ingested or integrated.

Slowly at first, and then with increasing speed as the years passed, each real atom, every concrete molecule, would first re-create and then replace itself with a luminous double. The old would slough off like so much dead skin.

I considered my actresses. As they responded to my questions with thoughtful postures, eyes closed or unseeing, I was consumed with a growing certainty.

They were *made* of light.

I hope I have caught some of that in this book, and that you will see and feel that magical quality as I did . . . the *light* that is in each of the great actresses in this book.

Actress to Actress is a salute—a salute from one actress to another.

Part One
STARS OF FILM

Grace Kelly

"**M**iss Gam, meet Miss Kelly," said a cameraman on the sound stage of "You Are There," the CBS TV show directed by my first husband, Sidney Lumet. We nodded briefly. I would have been hard-pressed to recognize the woman who was to become one of the most sought-after actresses in Hollywood, a paradox of dazzling beauty and patrician reserve. Where was the spark that would fire the imagination of the world? In her prim skirt, cotton shirt, flat-heeled shoes, and spectacles, she looked that day in the early 1950s like a small-town high school teacher with the sniffles. Her corn-silk hair was pulled back into a pontytail and her face was scrubbed clean except for a smidge of lipstick. She was even shy.

But the inner Grace turned out to be quite different. As our friendship grew, her personality began to reveal itself. Her strong determination to succeed as an actress was always tempered by inner calm and patience, qualities I felt must have come from her religious schooling. That and her acceptance of the world as it really is were unique in someone that young.

Grace and I had had parallel careers as models in New York, though our paths never crossed. Like many aspiring actresses we had taken up modeling temporarily. There was always the question of making a living, and, although she came from a wealthy Philadelphia family, Grace too wanted to pay her own way. Models made twenty-five dollars an hour then.

The young Grace Kelly (1952). By courtesy of Frank Kresi, Consul of Monaco.

We both made the circuit of TV drama in the golden days of television's infancy. We did "The Lux Video Theatre," "The Somerset Maugham Theatre," and "Robert Montgomery Presents." We were both included in a *Life* magazine article, "TV Leading Ladies." Grace was pictured in fishnet stockings as a sexy music-hall singer; I was "the face that thinks," the bad girl in whodunits.

Our movie careers, too, began at about the same time. While Grace and Audrey Hepburn fulfilled the 1950s dream of the vulnerable, witty princess who never swallowed her pride and always got what she wanted, I was tapped for the half-castes, suffering virgins, and *femmes fatales.*

Friendships can be based on mutual failings as well as mutual strengths. We had both been rejected for admission to Bennington College; both of us were poor cooks. We were both easily diverted by extraneous things, but Grace was more straightforward and single-minded. She had a general's sense of timing, knew when to strike and when to retreat, and always devised superb strategies. But it took me a while to discover what lay beneath the surface. To the end, the real, bubbling Grace was reserved for intimate friends.

Together we survived the rigors of studio life during the day and Tinsel Town's dangerous nights. More than once we would rescue each other from boredom and from potentially embarrassing situations. And through it all—we laughed.

Our friendship really started in 1954, when I checked into the Beverly Hills Hotel to start shooting a movie about Attila the Hun. Immediately, I suffered an attack of loneliness.

What was I doing in this tropical luxury mart? I went for a swim, joining the vulgar display of Hollywood's finest female flesh, oiling, turning, and seducing for a crack at the big time. It depressed me.

The next morning, for about one moment, I decided to quit Hollywood and take the next plane home. But the telephone rang and a friendly voice said, "It's Grace Kelly here. Why don't you come around for coffee this afternoon?"

In her private life, Grace was instinctively a homemaker and, given one room in Hollywood or a palace, she had the knack of transforming it into "Gracie's place," complete with inspired clutter. Much like its tenant, the apartment was very personal, feminine, and sentimental, filled with snapshots, sketches, and souvenirs from her first films. Everywhere there were pictures of her family. As she poured coffee, we compared notes about our separate African adventures; she had just returned from Central Africa, where she filmed *Mogambo,* and I from North Africa, where I had filmed *Saadia* for MGM.

Even though we had been thousands of miles apart, we had both taken endless pictures of laughing native children and rear views of their mothers. And then, of course, there were our rocks, all those incredible amethyst-veined stones that had looked so appealing in Africa and were strangely out of place in Hollywood's cardboard apartments.

"But what are we going to do with them *now?*" Grace asked, wide-eyed. Her ability to laugh at herself was one of her most appealing qualities. I saw it that day for the first time.

We talked about our wanderlust and the conflict between the drive for perfection in our work and the kind of life we both ultimately wanted to live.

I didn't mention my loneliness, but she must have sensed my turmoil and said, "Wouldn't you like to move in here?"

So I left the Beverly Hills Hotel, the home of myths and deals, and moved into the small apartment on Sweetzer Avenue in West Hollywood.

Since neither of us had gone to college, the roommate routine was new to both of us. For me, at any rate, it worked out comfortably and congenially. One reason we got along so well was that temperamentally we were so different. Grace never lost control. I found her very calming.

The apartment house where Grace and I lived was a square, ugly building of the 1930s, complete with a kidney-shaped swimming pool. Our neighbors were expensive ladies of the evening; early each morning, as we set out for our studios, they waved to us as they got out of their convertibles, handbags stuffed with fifty-dollar bills.

It was pleasant to come back in the evening and talk shop with Grace. I spent the day in my Max Factor-mahogany skin, and Grace was all pink and white as the heroine in Alfred Hitchcock's *Rear Window*. While she was exhausted from a day of serious acting, I was sore from having ridden horses through fire.

We would exercise every night, or at least make a stab at it— Grace in the bedroom, I in the living room. We always assured each other we'd keep it up for the prescribed fifteen minutes—until one night I quit early (not for the first time) and walked in on Grace to find her on her bed, fast asleep.

During the week all we managed to do in the early morning was grab our coffee, and in the evenings it was a quick hamburger before rolling into bed to learn lines for the next day. I was always the first one to use the bathroom at night—where I soaked for an hour in detergent to get the dark body makeup off. Then I came out as shriveled as a prune. By the time Grace got to bed, I would be asleep.

On weekends we lived it up. On Saturday mornings there was household shopping. Grace was thinner than I, but the battle of the bulge was never far from our minds. Even so, we stuffed ourselves with Grace's classic tomato spaghetti and my homespun beef Stroganoff, not to mention chocolate éclairs and strawberry cheesecake, washed down with champagne. Always champagne. Grace loved it, so we always kept some on ice. Then we would diet, mostly on prunes.

Grace Kelly at a press conference, before sailing the Constitution for Monaco for her wedding to Prince Rainier III. By courtesy of Frank Cresi, Consul of Monaco.

We both liked to take long walks, with no particular destination in mind, though when we sauntered forth in Hollywood or Beverly Hills we were courting arrest. In the kingdom of the car, walking the streets was practically a criminal offense.

Looking back, we were terribly naïve, considering that the world saw us as glamorous movie stars. We were working hard, but we played, like Nancy Drew and her pals, in a more innocent time, even in the loopy, hyped-up enclave that was Hollywood.

How did Grace differ from other actresses? There were some who saw nothing on film but a pretty, awkward, and inexperienced young actress who had a tentative grasp of characterization. How then could she hold an audience enthralled? Was it by her light convent-schoolgirl voice? The cool touch of aristocracy?

It is commonplace to say the appeal of an actress is mysterious, but the memory she has left in the hearts and minds of her audience is indisputable. Everyone was soon in the grip of her cool goddess looks and her apparent vulnerability.

Grace herself was always reaching for the necessary tools of her craft—technique that would lay to rest the controversy about her talent. She was "learning" in public. She never stopped trying to play with superior actors and trying to land a play on Broadway in which she could grow. (She never did get that play.)

Even though in her own words she called her talent "promising," hers were the concerns of any serious artist. But like her sisters, her ambition knew no bounds. Though Grace had many qualities that could have made her a fine "repertory nun," dedicated and ever willing, playing everything and growing old in the service of art, her cool elegance covered a depth of passion that spurred her toward stardom.

She has been quoted as saying, "I don't want to dress up a picture with just my face; if anyone starts using me as scenery, I'll return to New York." But that was unlikely once Hitchcock's passionate professional interest took hold. He was able to tap into her romantic and slightly fey sense of humor and bring out her banked fires of sensuality. After three Hitchcock pictures, both her technique and beauty grew.

Grace was always sensitive about the parts she lost in the theatre. She felt bad about Helen Hayes's rejection of her for *Wisteria Trees* and José Ferrer's use of Arlene Dahl instead of her as Roxanne to Jean Dalrymple's *Cyrano de Bergerac*. Her inner motor, which chugged along at full steam in films, never was fully developed for the stage. José Ferrer is reported to have said, after her reading for the City Center production of *Cyrano*, "Wouldn't someone tell the girl to talk louder?"

We were invited to many of the "Group A" parties, where your status depended on your rating with Louella Parsons. Admission to the group was based solely on money and power—movie currency. Grace was the reigning ice queen and "great box office"; I was her zippy brunette, "potential box office" friend.

On Saturday we were sitting around waiting to go to a late-evening party at Sam Goldwyn's when agent Charlie Feldman called. Grace disliked answering the phone, so I picked it up.

"May I speak to Grace Kelly, please?"

"Hi, Charlie. It's Rita Gam here."

Without a second's hesitation, Charlie replied, "Well, I'll be damned. How are ya, Rita? I'm having a dinner tonight. How would you two girls like to come along? I'll send a car over to pick you up at seven." Out of the corner of my eye I could see Grace signaling frantically, and I got the message.

"Charlie, we'd love to come, but we'll drive ourselves over. Is it dressy?"

There was a fractional pause as he hemmed and hawed: ". . . Well . . . sort of medium."

Smart Grace! Come seven, we drove up Benedict Canyon in Grace's mustard Chevy and arrived at Charlie's to find that there were no other cars in the driveway. We looked at each other as a discreet butler led us past two dim chandeliers in the hallway and then into the living room.

Then we met "the party"—Francisco (Baby) Pignatari, the South American playboy, and our host, Charlie Feldman. The gentlemen stood there in all their sunburned glory, smelling of expensive cologne and dressed in slick, expensive casual clothes and cashmere sweaters. They looked rather like plastic dummies from Bloomingdale's menswear department.

"Where's the party?" I asked innocently.

"This is it," Charlie replied, beaming.

The evening proceeded to go downhill from there. Grace sat up straighter and straighter behind her glasses and poker face. As the dinner progressed, we both noticed that the lights were getting dimmer and dimmer, and by the time we had finished the *coq au vin* Pignatari's hands were groping my knees.

"Let's go," I whispered to Grace in a panic.

"Let's wait for dessert—it might be good," she whispered back.

It was nine o'clock by the time we finished the coffee soufflé, and the room was almost dark. That's when Grace took over. Flashing one of her most brilliant smiles, she announced, "We're terribly,

terribly sorry, but we have to go on to another party."

Before the astonished men could catch their breath, we were out the door and into the Chevy, on our way to the Goldwyns'.

One time, a few days before Christmas, we two transplanted easterners were commiserating on our exile in the land of palm trees when songwriter Sammy Cahn invited us to a Christmas party. We dressed to the nines, Grace in a long green satin dress and pearls and, of course, her inevitable white kid gloves. Again, we drove ourselves there in Grace's old Chevy. Everyone murmured admiringly as she drifted up to the buffet table—she looked so fresh, so elegant and ladylike. But when we hit the dessert table, she plunged into the cake like a starving sailor. "Just one teeny piece for Christmas," she said as she wolfed it down. She was usually party-shy, but this night she was the hit of the evening, from her astrological predictions to her staged hypnosis of me to stop smoking. At one point, we were seated around the piano while Mitch Miller played Christmas carols. When Grace, Judy Garland, and I did a barbershop rendition of "Silent Night," someone muttered uncharitably, "The three graces." Quick as a wink, Grace quipped, "Will the real Grace please stand up?" Which she then did, bowing ceremoniously to that jaded group with one of her heart-stopping smiles.

My next film took me to Europe, so we gave up the apartment. By the time I got back, Grace and I hadn't been in touch for months. We had both been busy, totally occupied with our own films and our own romances. About that time Grace was being courted by dress designer Oleg Cassini, a suave man-about-town. Oleg had been dancing attendance for some months, but Grace had not said "yes" to him.

When she called me after New Year's Eve and invited me to a cocktail party to meet her intended, she also asked me to be a bridesmaid at her wedding. I thought she was going to marry Oleg.

"Rita, darling, won't you come and meet my prince?"

I accepted with great joy, assuming "my prince" was just her romantic way of referring to Oleg. I was truly expecting to see him by Grace's side, but, to my surprise, her prince was a real one.

Ranier showed up with a solitaire diamond ring "as big as the Ritz," as Grace described it. It was a long way from Sweetzer Avenue, and Grace and I hugged and I wished her a world of happiness. I knew that, though our friendship would remain, our lives would never be the same again.

Grace Kelly as the princess in Frederick Monar's The Swan *(1956). By courtesy of Frank Cresi, Consul of Monaco.*

In the years following her marriage, Grace and I still managed to see each other two or three times a year, sometimes more often—in Europe, whenever work took me there, or New York, when she made one of her frequent trips home to see her family in Philadelphia. One weekend I remember in particular—it was in 1962, following the Berlin Film Festival, where I had won best-actress award for my role in *No Exit*. I stopped in Monaco to spend a few days with Grace. Her excitement over my success typified all that was so special about her. But I sensed behind her loving and generous celebration a tinge of actor's envy. Throughout her married life her aspirations lay dormant because it would be unseemly for a Serene Highness "to act"; but her love of acting never flagged.

I remember her radiance the last time I saw her, in Philadelphia. Although she had a cold, she enjoyed being feted by old friends like Jimmy Stewart and Frank Sinatra and all Philadelphia in their "Tribute to Grace Kelly, Actress." How she loved being an actress!

Grace was finally finding her way back to acting. Eight days before her tragic death she wrote me a letter telling me she was very excited about doing a "poetry programme September 28th at Windsor in England at S. Georges Chapel and then would join Sam Wanamaker for a little tour of four cities to find some well-heeled donors for the Globe Theatre project in London."

Her craft may never have caught up with the size of her fame, but Grace's gaze was always focused on wide horizons, and an audience when not being amused by her charm undoubtedly felt that spirituality which was very much a part of her own private universe.

The loss of Grace moved me in so many ways, especially whenever I think of her as an actress. I don't believe the public's perception of her ever altered. As Princess Grace of Monaco she was still an actress, doing what actresses do, communicating, reaching out, fulfilling the heartfelt desires of a fantasy-starved world.

Jeanne Moreau

"**M**ost people don't have the energy for sex, so they give up and go to the movies," said Jeanne Moreau when she was the high priestess of French cinema.

Sitting in luxurious quarters high above Manhattan in New York's Parker Meridien Hotel, legs in a wide second position, arms akimbo, and hands moving expressively in front of her, Jeanne was talking excitedly. We were having a meeting about the possibility of making the Anaïs Nin novel *A Spy in the House of Love* into a film.

Despite the early-morning sunlight there was a cabal-like atmosphere in the twenty-third-floor hotel suite. Moreau, wearing a red housecoat like the robe of office for the head of a female coven, was talking with the electric passion that you would expect from New Wave's interpreter of romantic obsessions.

British writer Penelope Gilliatt *(Sunday, Bloody Sunday)*, my co-producer, Roberta Haynes, and I were all talking at the same time. But it was Moreau with her quick grasp of abstract ideas who zeroed in on the problems of filming *A Spy in the House of Love*.

The novel had been offered to her in the fifties as an acting vehicle. It never flew. Thirty years later we were presenting it to her as a possible project to direct. We were discussing the actresses who could play the part. Jill Clayburgh, Debra Winger, Meryl Streep, Jessica Lange . . . "Yes, yes, Jessica Lange—she is perfect, perfect," Jeanne said. "But what is the real meaning of *A Spy in the House of*

Love? Today who gives a damned about a woman, a neurotic woman who sleeps around? That may have been brave in the forties and fifties, but today zat means nothing."

Her words poured out—enthusiastic, original, intense. I could not take my eyes off her. I was mesmerized by the balletic movement of her hands. Beneath the exterior of this plumpish French hausfrau I could still see the intellectual darling, the mischievous sensualist of New Wave cinema. Charismatic without a doubt: compelling—that was the word.

She suggested that she make some instant coffee, but nobody wanted her to move—such was her charm and the urgency of the conversation.

The telephone rang several times but Jeanne ignored it. Then, after an hour of heated discussion we decided to discard *A Spy in the House of Love:* it was too dated, too old-fashioned in its concept of this woman as a sensual victim, a lost seeker. We decided that Penelope would fashion an original story, a suspense story, more relevant to the eighties. In the flush of excited communication we settled on a modern love story with the classical conflict—a woman caught between the love of two men. It would be a modern *Casablanca . . .*

It would be pure adventure—a story of passion set against a Middle Eastern background. Penelope argued for the use of Turkey, but we all felt that this would be not only difficult but dangerous as well. We all knew Morocco and loved it, so we settled on that.

Many "darlings" later we gathered up our winter coats and set a date to meet in Paris to discuss it further.

We waited for the development of the treatment.

We waited and waited.

When Roberta and I met Jeanne in a gray Paris two months later, complications had arisen and our hopes, like so many other well-intentioned film projects, had begun to slip away.

La Lumière, which is the French term for "lights, action, camera," was Jeanne's first directorial effort. In it she displayed insight, grace, and sensuality with the same authority behind the camera as she did in front of the camera. It mirrored many of her growing feminist beliefs and revealed haunting cinematic innovations.

She directed the other women in the film as well as herself with adult appreciation for the sympathetic detail, showing ways in

Jeanne Moreau, Eva (1965).

which people have meaning for each other outside of sexual relationships.

La Lumière unfolds with depth and lyrical organization in a series of encounters.

The star, Sarah, confident, acclaimed, pursued by younger men, tells her story and that of three other women who seem to be part of her egocentric personality.

The film is about the relationships of these women, all of different ages—to their families and their art. Like Jeanne, the film is both sensual and intellectual and about the needs of both men and women. She has a strong sense of life and a visual sense that explodes the essence of a character. For her heroine, Sarah, she projects sensuality, indolent sterility by a headboard made up of a fearsome collection of small primitive knives—too obvious, too Freudian a symbol of Sarah's inability to love, but mighty effective.

Moreau's attention to the small detail is very much in the tradition of all great filmmakers. Her search for truth moves her away from the obvious. She said, "It's not because you show a great orgasm in detail that you are true to facts. The mind has to be involved as well as the body."

La Lumière is really about friendship rather than love. Moreau thinks of friendship as being "less violent, more subtle than love. It expresses itself in small details that are not necessarily exciting. Love is such a mysterious thing to deal with that it has been replaced in many movies by sex, which is of course far simpler to portray. Women are less concerned with violence than men." Jeanne feels that profoundly, and being a woman and an artist has allowed her to express all that is natural in her soul.

"I am influenced by everything—directors, writers, even the sunset," she said wistfully.

Roberta and I felt that collaboration between her and British writer Penelope Gilliatt, who wrote an illuminating profile of her for *The New Yorker* magazine, would result in a fine film, true to the classical tradition of French films.

In her acting Morcau has always been articulate and sensitive to women's needs. She realized even before the crusade for women's liberation that men ran the film industry and that the films that brought her stardom like *Jules and Jim, Diary of a Chambermaid, La Notte, Les Amants,* were statements of how men felt about women. "More and more, now," she said with unique depth of understanding, "men are afraid to write about women. I think it's a reaction that is very truthful. Until now everything has been expressed through the eyes and sensitive feelings of men."

Moreau made her dramatic presence felt on the stages of the Comédie-Française and the Théâtre Nationale Populaire. Then she went on to make two dozen quite ordinary films. But in true film-diva style, when she fell in love with director Louis Malle, he became her first real film mentor, and her presence exploded on screen. His film *The Lovers* finally propelled her into the international fame that was to last decades.

She once explained in a *New York Times* interview, "When you start filming you're in a dangerous zone. It's like being on a raft in the middle of the ocean. You feel that the person in charge has tremendous power, and can order many things that would not be possible on dry land."

At the same time that Marilyn Monroe was making cute remarks like "I only wear Chanel No. 5 to bed," Jeanne was giving interviews that were concerned with woman as a natural and glorious creature. She made provocative and intellectual statements like "Being an actress and being a woman has never been a split for me. The thing that has been most valuable to me all my life is a taste for life itself.

"If a woman is not ashamed of being a woman she develops a close relationship with life through her body. When you have the pleasure of being a woman, you are in constant touch with earthy natural things like the cycles of the moon. All these strange movements that go on in a woman's body, the fact that she can give birth, it's incredible when you think about it. . . ."

She had to struggle to become an actress in an era of sex symbols, she fought and succeeded in giving many human and revealing performances.

I cherished her wonderful modern heroine in *Jules and Jim*. She brought the enigmatic smile to a high point of artistry at the time when it was just a fashionable convention. Michèle Morgan, Simone Signoret, Arletty, all used it. Seduction was impossible without it. But hers suggested eternity: a flash, a whisper of that smile before she died at the end of *Jules and Jim* will always stay with me.

In quick succession she made *The Trial* and *Les Liaisons Dangereuses*.

"After a crying scene it sometimes is difficult for her to stop crying," Louis Malle once said by way of explaining her technique as an actress. "Jeanne is the kind of actress who must build up into a scene. She is not at her best in the early takes. She might be worked up to a high pitch before I get what I want. But then, what comes out is pure magic. It is as though she were trying to repress feelings that for her are only too real."

While Hollywood films were made to formula, Jeanne Moreau's films had nothing to do with those conventions. When Louis Malle and Jean-Claude Carrière wrote scripts, they took into account the facets of her life and talents and molded a character about whom she already knew a great deal.

"I believe that every experience in a woman's life is valuable to her as an actress," Moreau said when she was at the height of her power as an actress. "When I portray something on stage or screen, some character, passion, or feeling—I must dredge something out of my own life to help make it real. But then, after stimulating the feeling for an audience, that feeling becomes an important part of my complete knowledge of myself. Therefore, it is impossible to say that such a thing comes from Moreau the actress or Moreau the woman. They cannot be separated."

Jeanne Moreau and Henri Serre in François Truffaut's Jules et Jim *(1963).*

Traditionally, France is chauvinistic and does not easily accept a woman as a director. Moreau's transition from world-class sex symbol to director was not easy. Only Orson Welles encouraged her to storm the male-dominated bastion. He was one of the first directors to appreciate her uniqueness as the sensual gamine; he was the first to encourage her to direct. "When it becomes painful for you *not* to direct, *then* do it," said Welles, the director's director.

She worked as a leading lady for an impressive list of the world's great directors: Roger Vadim, Michelangelo Antonioni, Peter Brook, Marcel Ophüls, Luis Buñuel, Tony Richardson, Jean Renoir, Phillippe de Broca, Orson Welles, and certainly the late François Truffaut, who captured all her magnetism as an actress and made her the pinup girl of the intellectuals. With the first film she directed, *La Lumière,* she joined their ranks. And now they have become her admiring peers.

L'Adolescent, directed and co-written by Jeanne Moreau, was her second film. It opened with the classic shot of a young girl watching Bastille Day celebrations in Paris in 1939 and closed in a small village in southwest France. It was there that a young girl and her grandmother, played by Simone Signoret, lived out their mysteries of womanhood and female wisdom.

Moreau said about her actors, "I know when something is painful. That is what directing is about. It is a process of growth that cannot be resisted. But when you talk in terms of artistic creation, the permission, the creation comes not from the society, but from within oneself."

Moreau has developed the ability to work on several levels at the same time. Her training as a woman taught her not to aspire to a job that was threatening to men, but to consider it to be a block she had to hurdle. As she achieved success, she developed the ability to work with men on every level, both as an actress and as a director.

I enjoyed my meetings with Jeanne enormously and regretted the end of our association. A flurry of transcontinental telephone calls kept our project alive for awhile, but unfortunately it finally collapsed. Wrong team, wrong subject, not enough story . . . The film died an aborted but graceful death.

Jeanne has a wonderful mind, rich, inventive, and original. But I am not sure that her time has come as a contributing director. In

France as well as in the United States women have not quite made it in a man's world, and her directorial career has been aborted by ancient prejudices. Men don't give money easily to back a woman's talent, longings, and technique unless they prove to be lucrative. Jeanne's first two pictures weren't financial winners. I hope future projects will be otherwise.

During our last meeting in her small, bright, and tidy apartment in Paris, she moved like a middle-aged Parisian Tinker Bell. She spilled light. In a kaleidoscope of newly lit cigarettes and bounding ideas she shared her very special gift of wisdom in a spotlight of her own making. As she talked with all her senses, it seemed to me that the generosity of spirit that belongs to her was best expressed by Picasso when he said, "People don't get older, they get riper . . . in a life where love is still the greatest refreshment of all."

Susannah York

"Why do people act, why do I? What's the impulsion?" asked electric Susannah York, the beauty whom *Life* magazine once described as "a bird for all seasons." "More than for glory and money, more than for glamour and for highs or escape. We act to understand." she said. "The impulsion is twofold. Through scrutiny to affirm ourselves and our emotions, recognize ourselves and people we know, and perceive by the struggle of will and imagination to learn of others. It is this deep-rooted curiosity about human beings and human behavior and the desire to share these findings that drive actors to invade or be invaded by one character after another."

Clad in a fuzzy pink sweater, she leaned her elbows on her kitchen table, her Goldilocks hair loose and flowing. Eyes followed her King James spaniel as he romped in a tangled Peter Rabbit London garden, and she repeated her definition of acting. "To act is to be invaded by one character after another."

I watched her carefully as she brewed coffee from fresh-ground coffee beans; she could have been any South London housewife but for her penetrating blue eyes and the dramatic shine to her voice. Glimpses of the "cuddlesome" baby-faced blond of the sexy sixties were visible as she talked on the phone about a benefit for an antinuclear movement. Susannah once said she was "afraid of time." One look at this lovely British actress and her competent dealing with the insistent telephone, this lady who came to world attention

as a girl in the seventies in the Alec Guinness–John Mills classic
Tunes of Glory, and I knew she had nothing to fear. "Time" has been
her friend.

In what seemed to be one breath, without a change of pace,
she put the phone down and switched the subject to her childhood.

Born in London in 1939, Susannah spent the later part of her
childhood with three sisters on a farm in Troon Ayrshire, not far
from the sea. Her family had moved to Scotland after the war;
while there she developed an early interest in painting and wrote
little plays to perform in their farmhouse. When she was fourteen
they moved back to London.

"I had a pony and a bike and even at six years I dreamed of
being an actress," she told me. "I started writing plays at seven, and
at nine I remember standing on a chair and announcing to the
world, 'I'm going to be an actress, a terrific actress, when I grow
up.'"

Her mother was "strong and beautiful and very spoiled"; her
father was a man of many talents, "a banker and a dreamer." Sitting
on top of a London bus, "a red London bus" she used to fantasize
about what it would be like to "be other people, the children going
to school, the secretaries and the workmen, and the city gentlemen
in their finely tailored suits." She would visualize their lives, where
they lived, and how they behaved at breakfast. "My life was a constant exploration—a becoming; I just wanted to *become* those other
people."

She said it had been "absolute magic" the first time she acted
and got her first laugh. She was nine then, and wanted to be a nurse
in a leper colony, an astronaut, and many other things when she
grew up. "But," she said, "when I played the ugly sister in
Cinderella and got a laugh leaving the stage with the boy who was
playing the other ugly sister, I knew from that moment that I could
only be an actress. I also realized that the ugly sister was a better
part than Cinderella's and I stopped being furious—proving, as
someone wisely said, that the 'snake has all the good lines.'"

After winning school prizes for biology and Latin and science,
she went on to win a scholarship at the Royal Academy of Dramatic Art. Ebullient and enthusiastic as only Susannah could be at
seventeen, she started a lifelong struggle to channel that energy, to
learn technique, to contain her enthusiasm. "It was quite a shock,"
she said. "Acting is the achievement of spontaneity," she continued.

Personal photo of Susannah York (1966).

"It's a horrible process of pulling the part apart, after you've given a smashing reading, till you're down to a pile of rubble. Then gradually building it up again."

When playing Nora in Ibsen's *A Doll's House* in her last term at the Royal Academy of Dramatic Art, she was asked by her teacher, Mary Wells, to stay after rehearsal. "Now, Susannah," said Mary Wells, "we're going through the scene again when Nora comes in loaded with sweetmeats and parcels, and you go through the door; when you unwrap the sailor suit, *really* unwrap it. We'll do it thirty times tonight." Susannah told me, "I thought I'd go berserk, but I learned that on each word and line there was a place to put down, unwrap, to run to the door, rush to the window, and turn back for a macaroon. Ms. Wells totally orchestrated that first page and a half. Nora became a child, a squirrel, and the quick and darting person that I really am. Instead of coming out totally different every time, I learned to repeat it and still be totally spontaneous."

She said of her performance in the record-breaking classic film *Tom Jones,* where she played glowingly opposite Albert Finney, that "it was a romp. My part was light comedy; it was also my first experience with improvisation, which shook me a bit."

About *A Man for All Seasons* with Paul Scofield, she confessed to being insecure and disagreeing a lot with director Fred Zinnemann. But the result was flawless.

Susannah keeps a journal in which she writes the case history of each character. She builds the character through a process she calls "diggability," carefully putting together the details and discovered facts. W. H. Auden once said, "How do I know what I think until I hear what I say?" Susannah said, "Till I read what I say or till I write it."

She writes in order to know. The portrait of a character emerges from her exploration. When she goes to rehearsal, she doesn't sit around and talk; she wants to get up and do it. Her research feeds the colors of her character; the more she knows, the more she does.

Acting is "an exploration of different characters," she said. "I stitch them, I make patchwork quilts, there are bits of me and bits of someone else, I drop out bits of me and add someone else, and so on. I used to find it was like a glass ball that had been dropped and was in smithereens, but it's the assembly after you've started breaking up that's important. Finding moves that seem correct and using what you are given by the other actors." She feels she is not instinctively a technical actress and she has to work very hard. Her bottom line is to be both strong and vulnerable. She feels that the only kind of stardom to fight for is Jeanne Moreau's brand, which takes a courage, a commitment, "on a grand scale."

Among the directors she has worked with are Fred Zinnemann, Sydney Pollack, Tony Richardson, and Ronald Neame. John Huston, who directed her in *Freud* opposite Montgomery Clift, said that Susannah, after sleeping only two hours a night and working round the clock opposite Montgomery Clift for five months, was one of the truly brilliant actresses of our time. Perhaps because of her beauty, or in spite of it, she chose her parts with care. When she did *They Shoot Horses, Don't They?* with Jane Fonda, before the picture started she fought for a rewrite, and throughout the filming, despite threats of lawsuits, she continued to fight.

True to her outspoken image, she played the part of Alice in *The Killing of Sister George* when she was twenty-seven. The story was about a triangular relationship, a marriage if you like, which happened to be Lesbian. She told me: "I felt it never made up its mind whether it was going to be a study of abnormal relationships or whether it was going to be a great comedy—in which case why the Lesbian thing?"

She approached the part as she would have worked on a stage performance—pen in hand, research and homework done.

She said of Alice that the problem was to individualize her and make her archetype come alive. "I stripped her of all labels," she said. "I thought of her as an insecure creature who was slack. Not purposely bad, just slack."

She held nothing back and allowed herself "total vulnerability."

It was "nerve-wracking," she said; she felt stripped—mentally and emotionally. "When Coral Brown and I did the explicit love scene, it was difficult to be naked in front of the all-male crew. But more important than my discomfort was my willingness to be sexually implicit."

Her brilliance showed in this fine interpretation; it was courageous, insightful, and complex.

When she played Hedda Gabler at the Roundabout Theatre in New York, she was struck by the immediacy of Ibsen's writing, noting during rehearsals that nothing was premeditated with Hedda's character. Each action erupted out of the last. For example,

Susannah York in Lock Up Your Daughters.

the act of giving the pistol to Lövborg and the burning of the manuscript were spontaneous to the character, not calculated or enigmatic acts. Hedda, she said, was constantly astonishing herself.

She said of Hedda: "She is terrible—full of terror and terrifying. She is a total outsider, a victim of her own nature, which is too big, too vital for her to deal with."

"I sort of become a part," she said in an interview with Andy Warhol in 1973, "and I jump out of it when life finally jolts me out. If I become too deeply involved, it becomes difficult to slough it off. It's painful but it's a part of life."

Susannah strongly believes that acting for the camera and acting on stage come from the same root. But everything Susannah does springs from passionate convictions. "When I want to walk away from someone I've been deeply involved with, it's difficult, but I do it, and the person one leaves always becomes a part of one; the same is true of leaving a part."

Our conversation turned to children and then to the impossibility of sustaining an ongoing relationship with a man.

Susannah flitted across the kitchen to get us another cup of coffee, lightly touching things as she went.

"What about children?" I asked. "And a mate?"

She appeared quite relaxed as she spoke of her son Orlando and daughter Sasha. "I'm a very domestic person. I love my house. I love my children. I like being here when they get off from school or picking them up from school or taking them to the dentist. I'm very involved in their lives and they in mine."

She said wistfully: "About a mate . . . well . . ."

Then we both spoke at once, with one voice, almost, about the difficulty of actresses having a long-term, long-standing relationship.

Ah, a mate!

"We're interested in those kinds of people who are doing precisely, exactly, what we are doing. My ex-husband was an actor with whom I went to acting school. We were perennial students. We were questers, seekers. The trouble came with the separations, the pressures of the new intimacies that were developed in our working lives. We are constantly involved in projects in which you get to know new people over a three- or four-week period, with an intimacy that in normal life would take you three to four years to build up.

"So the chips are down very early on. That kind of nakedness, that kind of vulnerability . . ." She sighed. "To find someone who is absolutely on your wave length . . . If you are lucky enough, if you can, just take care not to . . ."

Susannah's manner changed quickly. One moment she was flamboyant and the next she was deceptively gentle, shy, even, like her portrayal of Jane Eyre. There is also a streak of emotional exhibitionism in her, but always there is sincerity and a willingness to dare.

Perhaps Susannah, like Alice in *The Killing of Sister George,* was born out of her time. She seems to have the energy and commitment of a more passionate age. Perhaps her gamine, almost wanton image didn't fit in with what the public wanted. The great dramatic actresses of the time looked like Ingrid Bergman and Deborah Kerr.

Perhaps her intensity, which sometimes bordered on hysteria, frightened her peers and robbed her of a well-deserved place in the firmament of stars. All that should have happened for Susannah didn't, and great public favor and public identification have always somewhat eluded her. But I have always loved her spirit, her talent, and her willingness to share. Her view, almost mystic, was expressed in these words: "Acting is life happening to the actor, and conversely, an actor happening to life. The means of expression may alter, but the distillation remains the same. You use all you've learned to garden emotions for other people."

Susannah sighed and tossed her tousled blond curls. "I act," she said, "because it's the thing I do best. I act because it's my truth."

Shelley Winters

I have known Shelley for more than thirty years. We first got to know and like each other when we were nubile actresses in New York City and traded evening dresses for Saturday-night dates. After years of "girl talk," when we had this interview recently, we finally got serious about our work.

I have always been swept into Shelley's world within seconds, and upon her confessing that when she was still Shirley Schrift of Brighton Beach, Brooklyn, she would act in a clothes closet in the schoolroom or on a street corner, I began to listen intently.

Shelley stretched out on a well-worn couch, informed me that the chicken soup would be ready in a few minutes, and asked me to fire away.

"How did you feel about being a sex symbol?" I asked, "and how did you fight your way out of that corner?"

Shelley covered herself with a blanket and allowed her voice to rise hysterically twice in one sentence, a technique I've heard her use to advantage before, to catch the attention of an audience. "Aw, Rita," she said, "you know the answer to that one as well as I do." She mentioned the *National Enquirer* and the extraordinary circulation it had "because people got vicarious enjoyment from the idea of sexy movie stars. I tell you, Rita, it's quite an accident that I became a sex symbol. I wasn't particularly beautiful. If you look at my early films, I was sexy, with a kind of earthy sexiness. But Universal did the whole thing of bleaching my hair and making it into a chrysanthemum, then the eyelashes and those kinds of parts—I was sexy in a vacuum.

"A sex symbol, a sexual object, is really a character. Even Marilyn Monroe created that persona separate from herself. And Dustin Hoffman, in *Tootsie,* created a sex symbol and a character."

Her next book was going to be called *All Tributaries and No Streams* and would be devoted to her way of being an artist. She wants to explore the advantages of being an artist, how all actors use the traumas of their lives. Directors and teachers, she said, teach you how to use the human experience.

She got up to go to the kitchen to get the soup. She said as she walked, "I had a tumor when I was a child, in the days when they didn't explain anything to children. It was very strange, very unwomanly. When something like that happens to a girl child, you feel that you must be more sexy and more womanly than every other woman in the world. I think that's why I allowed myself to be used in publicity as a sexpot or whatever they called it in those days."

While precariously balancing two bowls of soup, she whispered "Soup's ready," and continued. She told me how, when she was young, she'd go out with someone who would be relating to Shelley Winters, the image created by Universal, with the pushed-out gold lamé bosom, the whole game they'd taught her to play. Today it's still there to a degree, she said. "I still do that; I don't know why. When I do Johnny Carson or Merv Griffin shows, I'm a middle-aged sex symbol. I've been trained to present myself that way. When they ask me those dopey questions I give them dopey answers. And think of all the distinguished roles I've played. Why? I think it's quite an accident that I became a sex symbol . . . I hate it."

"But I think people become actors," she said, "out of their need for love. They want the world to love them, and they try to twist an unsympathetic part around until they get that love." Shelley spoke of how she wanted to justify the part in *A Patch of Blue,* a part for which she won an Oscar. She very much wanted the audience to love and understand her even though she punched and blinded her daughter with acid. She used to "throw up every night" until director Guy Green said, "Just show us the woman and don't worry about what the audience thinks."

Hollywood became aware of Shelley in her performance as the

vulnerable tramp, a minor but memorable debut in *A Double Life* with Ronald Colman.

But the moment when she truly came into her own was on the night of November 9, 1955, when the curtain rose on Broadway on Michael Gazzo's *A Hatful of Rain*. It was then that Shelley's metamorphosis took place. As the reviews came ringing in with "Wonderful, heartbreaking, the birth of an affecting and effective actress," Shelley announced, "Please understand that I am through with this blonde bombshell business."

As a fellow actress I always appreciated her total belief in the role she's playing; that, along with her extraordinary concentration, is the secret of her talent. The character and Shelley become one. She says she is a slow worker. It takes her time to learn lines. Her peers have despaired when working with her. They called her selfish. Such is her dedication to the part, her identification so total that I am reminded of a more dangerous profession. When I watch Shelley act, she has something of the tightrope walker about her. You feel that if she went just an inch more, she would die right there in front of you.

The complexities in her personality are too numerous to analyze. But one thing is certain. She never stops giving, I suspect not even in her sleep. Her energy scatters like so much buckshot, and she is not always right or safe. One experience I had with Shelley a few years ago when we were living on the same block in Beverly Hills came dangerously close to making one too many demands on friendship. I got a telephone call at ten at night and Shelley, her voice desperate with need, said, "Save tomorrow night for dinner at the Beverly Hills Hotel." Quickly her tone changed to enthusiasm. "I've got the backing for *Snow Angel*." That was the play by Lewis John Carlino about a prostitute and Shelley wanted to make it into a film. "Get dressed up terrific; the man who's got the money wants to meet you."

We met in a private dining room in the Beverly Hills Hotel, the mecca of the well-heeled and well-oiled. Shelley and her small entourage were escorted in to dinner by the would-be producer, a three-hundred-pound gentleman whose attaché case filled with two million dollars was chained to his wrist.

The next day's *Variety* read: Con Man Entertains Favorite Movie Characters.

Shelley Winters, Night of the Hunter *(1955).*

As Shelley tells the story, and she has told it many times, with a straight face and naïve wonderment in her voice, the punch line is always, "I thought he was a nice guy, but I just couldn't take the money. How can you take money from a gangster?"

How had she learned her trade? I asked.

When she studied with Charles Laughton, she learned how to analyze scripts and "how to put my instrument into the character." She made the switch, she said, from being a personality to being a character.

When Shelley first worked at the Actors Studio, Lee Strasberg made his students do things from books—exercises. But, she insisted, "We had no responsibility to the text. We worked on our own instrument, on our imagination. Then we had to work on a character to fulfill the play." Once she saw Montgomery Clift do a scene in which he wore purple shoes. "What he did with it, I mean how he dealt with the purple shoes, was fascinating. I didn't know what the hell the scene was about but it was fascinating. *That's* technique." The technique of acting enthralled her.

"Someone said acting is pretending that you're not pretending. If you are cold, you make the audience feel cold. When you yawn on stage, the audience yawns with you. That's why it's dangerous to yawn on stage. You light up sensory things with your imagination. There is a magical thing. There's no play there until the audience is in their seats. You can't perform a play to an empty house. You need that audience to throw those vibrations back."

I encouraged Shelley to talk about the essential but difficult-to-describe charisma of great actresses. I wanted to know if she felt it could be developed. Shelley, whose own inner light can be seen a block away on a foggy day, said that Michael Chekhov taught her how to create it. She said that by touching objects on stage and creating electricity you could go off stage but still leave the impression of being there.

Shelley laughed and related how when once she did a television show with my ex-husband, director Sidney Lumet, he asked her to "Come in the door, turn on the light, go over to the couch and say your line."

"So I came in the door, I sat on the couch, and said the line," said Shelley.

Sidney said, "No, Shelley. You come into the room, turn on the light, you sit down, and say the line."

"So I came in the door. I stood there. I sat down and said my line."

He said, "Turn on the light, dumbbell."

She screamed: "I did!"

Then she smiled at me and said: "I thought he meant my *inner* light, and I was turning it on. That was the last time I worked for Sidney Lumet."

She began to speak about the audience. "If they don't laugh or cry, they twitch; they let out sibilant sounds, a sigh, all kinds of things . . ." She stopped for a moment, thought about the issue, and said vehemently, "I don't believe in the fourth wall. I'm *always* aware of the audience. Of course I pretend there's a fourth wall there, but there isn't. You really would be nuts if you believed it."

What about the Shelley Winters whose performances include the films *A Double Life, The Diary of Anne Frank, A Place in the Sun, Lolita, Alfie,* and the stage play, *A Hatful of Rain*? The Shelley whose craft has brought her four Oscar nominations, two Oscars, two Emmys, and a myriad of honors like the Golden Nymph (the solid gold award that Princess Grace gave her)?

She described how George Stevens would talk to the actors and how he could galvanize their emotions. Some of her greatest performances were helped by such shrewd direction. In *The Diary of Anne Frank* he would turn up the heat so that all the actors felt the suffocating atmosphere. In the winter scenes he'd turn on the air-conditioning full blast so that they "all practically died of pneumonia." And after each scene was shot he would play "The Purple People Eater" to relax everyone.

Shelley said: "He kept telling me that I was the most courageous person there. He would put on a recording of Hitler talking to his storm troopers and say, 'You're not frightened.' He showed us film of the piles of bodies, some alive, some dead. It's haunted me the rest of my life. It terrified me. I wish I hadn't seen it, but all that time he kept saying, 'Shelley, you're brave.' He evoked in me abject terror finding courage. The word ambivalent is very hard for actors to act out, but human beings are very ambivalent about many things. He pulled that out of me."

Her spectacular characterization in 1955 in *A Hatful of Rain* was the result of her years of fruitful study with Charles Laughton

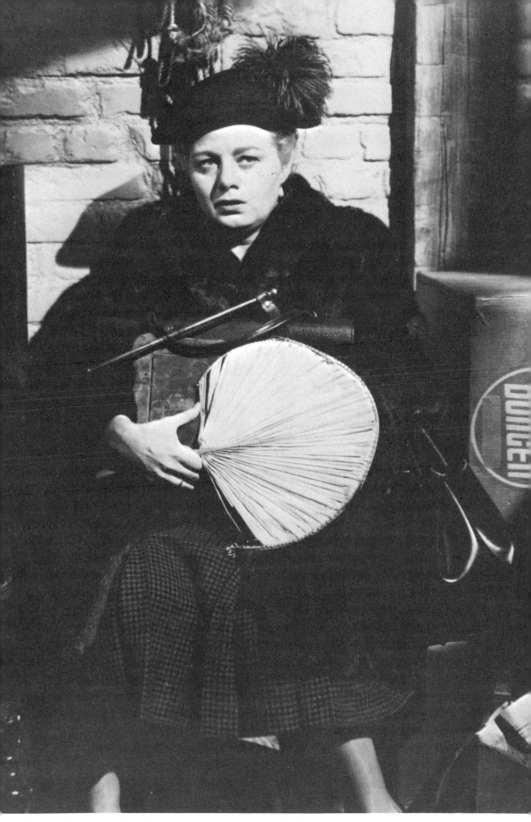

Shelley Winters, The Diary of Anne Frank *(1959).*

in his Los Angeles Workshop and with Lee Strasberg. Every movement was true to the framework of the character and also to her
own personality. She became the prime example of The Method.
But Shelley actually uses *all* methods to arrive at a character. "In
Lolita I had nothing in my frame of reference for the part. At that
time everything I played was within my frame of reference except
where I acted dumb. But she wasn't; she was a shrewd thing—but
she was unworldly and I certainly wasn't unworldly. She was nothing like me, but I knew a woman like her—rather shallow, someone
who joined book clubs but didn't understand what she was talking
about. I got it from the outside; I got it from a kind of effective
memory of that kind of person."

That process of dredging things up keeps her floating around
when the curtain comes down. This was one of the reasons, she
said, that so many actors are alcoholics or are on drugs or are overweight. Sometimes Shelley takes a Librium backstage after a performance and won't talk to anyone for an hour or so, so she can "come
down" from the performance.

Shelley is a mass of contradictions. With the help of twenty-five
years of in-house analysis she has tried to sort them out. She's a
worker, that's for sure, and as far as I can remember she's never
been without a project. She goes where the good roles are, and for
the last few years where *any* role is; today, Shelley is constantly
battling the bulge and her roles are limited by the size of her girth.

She says: "I've always felt that acting is as important as breathing. But it gets lonely going to bed at night with only statuettes for
company. You gotta make a choice, you gotta make your choice
. . . and I made mine."

Shelley has gotten everything she wanted from being a movie
star—fame, adulation, money, respect. "Actors are the royalty of
America," she once said. "I like everything about being an actress. I
like the fan letters, my bright red convertible, my mink coat and
stole, and the premieres. Most of all, though, I love acting." We
have only to remember her splendid performances in *A Place in the
Sun* and *A Hatful of Rain* to know why.

She can be full of generosity. I remember how she went out of
her way, when I was making *Sign of the Pagan* with Jack Palance for
Universal, to coach me on film acting, telling me to hold my
thought in a scene even if I had nothing to say and was in the back

of a shot. She advised me to keep my hair in the style that I had established in *The Thief* when I first became a star, so that the public would always recognize me. I took the first part of her advice but not the second—alas!

Her generosity extends to larger matters, too. I have seen her huge raw emotion move charity audiences into parting with millions of dollars for Israel.

After several hours of that winter afternoon's tête-a-tête, the non sequiturs were still filling the air. "I'll tell you, there's one thing you can say about living in a ghetto. It either makes you strong or it kills you. Eleanor Roosevelt once told me I'm an emotional Democrat. My heart's in the right place even though I'm a little weak on facts. I remember everything; I just don't know where everything is. I'm jealous of Brooke Shields. I would have liked to look like Brooke Shields. I'm jealous of Jessica Tandy; extraordinary actress and I love watching her. Sexuality! In *Streetcar Named Desire* Marlon Brando just wiped everyone off stage.

I couldn't resist asking, "Did you have an affair with Marlon?"

Shelley piped back, "None of your business. Just read my book. You obviously didn't even read it, much less memorize it. A good friend would memorize it. I'll give you a copy: read it."

Endearing, annoying, vulnerable, and hard-working and busy as a three-ring circus. On stage, in life, or on the screen you can't take your eyes off Shelley.

Shelley still hadn't run out of conversation by the time evening came, and I had run out of tape. She said, as I put on my coat and was moving out the front door, "Bette Davis is one of my role models. She always enchants me because she's not afraid to speak. Sometimes she'll do things, outlandish and outrageous, but always you see a fascinating and mercurial and interesting actress. Don't you think, Rita?"

A blast of cold night air hit me as I walked down Central Park West and I thought, yes, fascinating, mercurial, interesting—the same can be said about you, Shelley.

The Mavericks:
Jane Fonda, Jessica Lange, Vanessa Redgrave, Meryl Streep

What do Jane Fonda, Jessica Lange, Vanessa Redgrave, and Meryl Streep have in common besides being great film stars? They are all beautiful, bigger than life as the archetypical romantic heroines, and they all are embarrassed by abundant energy and intelligence. They are actresses in the tradition of Sarah Bernhardt. They are the mavericks.

Their lives are shot through with private peccadillos and public mistakes and still they are forgiven. They step out of the bounds observed by ordinary people and they get away with it. Star watchers, fans, and all the persistent guardians of public opinion continue, regardless of those stars personal eccentricities or outrageous rhetoric, to support them—unlike Ingrid Bergman, who paid for her transgressions by being banished from the American scene and screen.

When I first met Jane Fonda she was sitting at the feet of Lee Strasberg at the Friday session at the Actors Studio. She was clear-eyed, friendly, and ever watchful. It seemed she went from an ambitious ingenue to international sex symbol in a minute, and in even less time she became an outspoken political activist. She has the actor's gift of being a chameleon. Today the famous Fonda eyes of blue are still projecting droll humor even as they earnestly cajole a group of leotarded women to swing to her aerobic beat.

The French director's beautiful wife Jane, the futuristic Barbie doll Barbarella, have completely disappeared and have been replaced

Jane Fonda with her father, Henry. Courtesy of the Springer Collection/Bettmann Archive.

by the jogging wife of a Santa Monica politician. Jane has always seemed to me to be a kind of buccaneer, an adventuress who played on a broad field, using her talent to take her to places other women can't go. But it is the Jane Fonda of *Klute* that I like most.

When I played a lesbian call girl opposite her in *Klute,* there was a moment of brief but honest contact in our work together that I cherish. Director Alan J. Pakula developed a very special and interesting rhythm in our scene. He made sure we were relaxed even though there was chaos all around. He had hired real call girls and prostitutes for the nightclub scene, and while they were busy shooting up in the ladies' room, Jane and I were rehearsing our scene. Jane calmly fixed her attention on me; the world could have collapsed around us and we still would be there, such was her concentration, her grasp on the conflicted character of Bree. Jane has a beautiful acting instrument; her relaxation was total.

Jane and the private detective (Donald Sutherland) interviewed my character about the murders; I gave a long reply that helped them not at all and then Jane improvised a simple "Okay." It proved to be a brilliant moment and it projected a world of depth and resignation.

Jane Fonda, Julia *(1977)*.

Although I admire Jane in most of her civilian enterprises, I have wished on occasion that she would apply that same energy to finding and developing acting parts for that considerable talent of hers. There is a gallery of modern women she might give to us; she could do for our generation what Katharine Hepburn did for hers, both on stage and on film.

As annoying as my silent and sexy public image was for me after *The Thief,* Jessica Lange's sultry actress going ape over *King Kong* must have been for her. How did Minnesota-born Jessica Lange solve that sex-kitten problem? After many dispiriting years of Hollywood inactivity, it was with wit and intelligence and luck that she accomplished it.

Jessica has always been adventurous. She entered college as an art major, dropped out, and then crisscrossed the United States and South America. Settling briefly in New York to join a small modern dance company (an offshoot of Merce Cunningham's), she became engrossed in the study of mime and then went to Paris to live and continue her training under one of the greatest mime artists in the world, Étienne Decroux. That training shows in her work. Her acting seems effortless and without tension; thoughts come ringing out clearly and she has a subtle sence of characterization. She is a thoughtful actress.

Perhaps her peripatetic movements were due to her being a child of the 1960s, when protest was normal to the young of that era, but I suspect she would have been a maverick anyway. Jessica's life-style continues to be unconventional. Though unmarried, she has had two children—one with Baryshnikov, another with Sam Shepard.

Her creative promise started to bloom when Bob Fosse wrote her into *All That Jazz* in 1979 as the eternal femme fatale whom he called Death. Her performance was impressive, and thereafter her screen career took an unexpected turn for the better, allowing a considerable talent to expand and change and grow. In *Tootsie* she turned her dumb one-liners into ironic gems, but it was really in *Frances* that her ability to understand and to deal in a creative way with her own exceptionally broad emotional range gave to the public a haunting portrait of a woman in agony. And then, in *The Postman Always Rings Twice,* she projected an effortless sexuality that was like a second skin.

In *Country* she displays a firm and winning true grit, and in *Sweet Dreams* she shows the range of her talent for characterization when she plays the flamboyant country singer Patsy Cline.

What these roles confirmed is her unique ability to immerse herself in the life of a part. She said when she was making *Frances,* "I understand her abhorrence of authority. What happened to Frances Farmer could happen to me in my life. One or two things go wrong and snowball, and suddenly it's a real nightmare."

Empathy and courage are the words that come to mind to de-

Jessica Lange, The Postman Always Rings Twice *(1981).*

scribe Jessica Lange's considerable qualities, plus, of course, humor, the kind of wry humor that sings out in a crisis and makes her rapport with an audience complete and magical.

Vanessa Redgrave is today the most complex and perhaps most confusing example of current fame. She is a gloriously trained and exquisitely accurate actress. When I think of her as the Henry James heroine who walks bravely into a decadent world with a stride that takes my breath away, and then her personal and militant choice of political loyalties, angers me. I have to pause for a moment and try to make myself understand her particular genius.

Personal photo of Vanessa Redgrave. Courtesy of the Springer Collection/Bettmann Archive.

I first noticed and applauded this lanky lovely-looking actress in a small film called *Morgan*. Then, when I saw her ardent, pretentious and gloriously silly *Prime of Miss Jean Brodie,* the play, I was as moved as I haven't been since I was a child watching with wonder as Laurette Taylor floated above the stage in *Glass Menagerie.* From *Jean Brodie* on, I've waited eagerly for every Redgrave triumph. I wasn't disappointed when her seething, chaotic characterization of dancer Isadora Duncan came to the screen.

Vanessa Redgrave, The Trojan Women *(1972).*

It is therefore with much regret, born of personal prejudice, that I confess to seeing Vanessa Redgrave's current work with a jaundiced eye. We both made documentaries about the Mideast at the same time: mine was about the women of Israel; Miss Redgrave made a film for the Palestine Liberation Army, so violent in its intent that Israel wouldn't allow her to cross their borders.

Vanessa Redgrave is a wildly gifted woman. She can sing, she can dance, she speaks several languages, she rides a horse well, and how she can act! Perhaps her own words give a clue to her sometimes bizarre activism. "I don't picture myself acting forever and ever. But I sense that I have always been searching for something and have never found it. Somehow, whatever it is, I think I will find it in acting. Maybe not."

And I hope you do, Vanessa, I hope you do.

Meryl Streep is a maverick only in the sense that she refuses to follow the herd and to play the movie-star game, so much so that she has created her own rules of stardom.

When I saw the wedding scene in *The Deer Hunter,* I had the exhilarating sensation that I was watching the reincarnation of Carole Lombard as Robert De Niro swung a red-nosed and excited Meryl Streep around the floor in a polka. The same cool playfulness shone through her upper-middle-class detachment, a sense of joy that could explode at any moment into chaotic pain.

I became a Meryl Streep watcher, a fan. What seemed flawless reality really was expertly assimilated technique. I could imagine her as the eager first-year drama student at Yale who, blessed with a strong physical and mental constitution, would be the first in her class with her homework on script analysis.

In characterization, Streep is a gymnast. Her use of the tools of an actress is inventive and accurate. Her understanding of subtext is superb. Certainly no American actress today has her range or technique.

Streep is the kind of actress who researches a part with the thoroughness of a scientist. Her meticulous attention to detail gives depth to the most superficial part, but with the instinct of an artist she has said, "There is no speck of reasoning in a certain moment in *Sophie's Choice.* And as an actress I can't tell you why she does what she does. There is no logic, and that's the point." As much as she prepares for a part, Streep trusts her instincts and feels that spontaneity is the key. She thinks about a character and remains blank until she reacts as the character is written upon by her circumstances.

When I saw her performance as the gum-chewing lower-middle-class Karen Silkwood who blew the whistle on the plutonium plant after becoming alarmed about its safety standards, I realized just how remarkable her Sophie Zawistowska was. For the part she learned German and Polish and assumed such totality of character that I could watch the rhythm of her thoughts.

Not surprising is her understanding of the role that observation plays in the creation of a character. Her complaint about fame is not only that it impinges on her privacy, but that it robs her of the necessary anonymity to observe other people. They always seem to be watching her.

Streep has a capacity for transmitting extraordinary intensity of understanding between her and other characters. There is something about her, clear to other actors she has worked with, that she is acting for the whole film. She is what I think of as an actor's actor. Moments of some of her performances come to mind. I was haunted by her depression in the courtroom scene in *Kramer vs. Kramer,* her passion as the Victorian heroine in *The French Lieutenant's Woman,* her raw common humor as Karen Silkwood, and her clinging-vine fearful love in *Sophie's Choice.*

What alchemy does she use to define the differences between the soul of a Texas girl like Karen Silkwood and the wounded Polish refugee Sophie? How does she so completely and for every moment on screen think within her characters and embrace their emotional idiosyncracies so completely? Her intuitive understanding of the subtext of a script and her ability to make it her own combine to become the secret of her talent.

If this were still the more innocent thirties and forties she would be bringing to us civilized laughter and tears in one film after another; but we're in the hard-edged eighties, and the double-edged studio system is as dead as the assembly line and the carhop, so only Meryl Streep's good judgment and the skill of her agent nourish and protect her talent. The blonde, hazel-eyed actress is on her own to find good properties with only her instinct to guide her.

She can come up with a dud, as she did in *Falling in Love.* It was a poor choice of script to show her lighter side. But her radiance and rare comic sense showed through even so, particularly in the scene when she was dressing for her heavy muffin of a lover, Robert De Niro.

I think any actress who can look at the realities of a profession as difficult and corrupt as our film industry, and continue contributing unique and surprising performances is a heroine. She said of *Still of the Night,* a silly Hitchcock-style suspense thriller where she played a mysterious seductress who lured psychiatrist Roy Scheider through the streets of New York, "Who the hell cares? I'm not ashamed of what I did, but I wish we'd aim higher. People who are smart can just do something that they think will be popular because that's what's selling now."

Meryl Streep, The French Lieutenant's Woman *(1981).*

In *Out of Africa* she defines with almost witch-like accuracy the character of Danish novelist Isak Dinesen, again demonstrating her impeccable ear for the true sounds of her character.

I love her casual reference to the "business" as "a sports arena." I get the sense that a recurrent theme in her ongoing relationship to her work as art and her work as a public event is humor. But since the moment she was canonized on the cover of *Time* magazine as Magic Meryl, she has become defensive and slightly insecure about all the attention.

Blithe spirit, craftswoman, responsible citizen, all qualities surface with kaleidoscopic speed across her face. And also there is mystery, a blush, thoughts unspoken, wishes unfulfilled—the eternal woman.

If it is an actress's job to enrich the lives of an audience, these actresses more than fulfill their duty. I have only to think of Jane Fonda's look of disgust and resignation in *They Shoot Horses, Don't They?* Jessica Lange's frantically trapped eyes in *Frances*, Vanessa Redgrave's spiritual commitment and abandonment as Julia, and Meryl Streep wrapped in her dark cape against the winds of fate in *The French Lieutenant's Woman*.

In the words of Jane Fonda when she answered Oriana Fallaci's condescending statement, "I think you found a brain; the title of this interview should be 'The Birth of a Brain,'" Jane said, "Oh, no. I wouldn't put it like that, because it looks like someone who came from darkness to light. For me, it was more like going from confusion into focus, from vague floating thoughts and ideas and uncertainties and conflicts, to something very clear, very neat. Yes, the title should be 'I'm Coming into Focus.' And please, Oriana, should I die tomorrow, please tell them that I was not joking; that I was serious."

Perhaps what all these unique and beautiful actresses, the Mavericks, are doing is coming into focus in public. And happily I applaud not only their talent but their personal courage.

Part Two

THEATRE
VOICES

Julie Harris

"I measure every grief I meet with analytic eyes. I wonder if it weighs like mine or has an easier size." In her sweet and smoky voice Julie Harris quoted these lines from Emily Dickinson's poetry. Those words embody her life and her art.

Sitting in the garden of a Spanish house above the hills in Studio City, Los Angeles, I was having tea with Julie, an actress of special luminosity. Her Yorkie, Teresa, snuggled closer to her on the stone bench, and hummingbirds busily explored the California hibiscus. Low-flying planes accompanied her whispered thoughts. She sat straight as a British schoolgirl, head tilted at an inquiring angle, talking with the same poignant intensity that I remember her exhibiting twenty-five years ago when we did Lillian Hellman's *Montserrat* together on Broadway. She is now in the popular television series "Knots Landing," but there is a sense of isolation about her, as if she still lives under a glass bell.

Julie was born in Grosse Pointe, Michigan, a wealthy suburb of Detroit. She was the only girl, between two brothers. Her mother had a fourth child, a "blue baby" with the Rh factor, who died. When one listens to Julie talk about that, one feels that the loss of that child created a barrier between her mother and herself.

"My mother and I had a difficult, very difficult time together because she wanted somebody like Grace Kelly or Audrey Hepburn, and I was a disaster to her. I had my sort of Cinderella look and I was pathetic to her. She wanted to have my hair styled. No," said Julie, "I wasn't the daughter she would have wished for."

She said she always wanted her mother's approval, though—and since her mother was "star gazy" about the theatre, Julie was always pretending her paper dolls were actresses.

Julie had a particular sensitivity to the lost young women in the plays of Carson McCullers and John Van Druten. Could this be the reason? Julie said that her life was a series of mistakes, of stops and starts. She used to have terrible depressions and felt there was a lot of uncertainty inside her, which sometimes crept up and overwhelmed her with the question "What am I doing?"

My first awareness of Julie came when I saw her in the play *Sundown Beach,* directed by Elia Kazan. She exploded suddenly on the Broadway scene; almost overnight her name was spoken with admiration up and down the street. I'll never forget her in the play, standing mute on the far left end of the stage. She had a lovely tentative presence, a slim girl with long apricot-colored hair.

"I loved that part, I loved her sort of muteness. You know, her mute sorrow. I loved that play, and Elia Kazan, well, he was a mesmerist, a great director. He directed by secret innuendos. He surprised you. He had such a warmth and such charm. He wrapped you in it. You felt safe."

Could we trace her talent directly to those early years? We were quiet for a moment; I could feel the angel of silence passing overhead. Julie said, "I once heard an interview with Laurence Olivier and Dick Cavett. Olivier said, 'I inherited the wish to be an actor from my mother and father.' I thought, what a beautiful phrase, because it suggested how I felt. My father, when he was in college, was in the Yale Drama Club and acted in Shakespeare and in the classics, and mother absolutely adored the theatre and had some theatrical friends. I, too, inherited the wish from both of them—the excitement that they felt about the theatre.

"The first time that being an actress had any meaning for me was in a Christmas play I did, *The Jongleur de Notre Dame.* I was very emotional. And I thought, this is really something, to be able to move people. I didn't know what I had done. But it was exciting to feel at the center of everything."

I asked Julie what she felt was the keynote of her acting.

"The ability to be caught up in a story, to really believe in a situation. That's the power of belief."

Eleonora Duse was Julie's role model. Duse was an actress who really "believed" to an extraordinary extent. When she played Juliet

Julie Harris as Frankie Addams in Carson McCullers's The Member of the Wedding *(1949). Courtesy of Julie Harris.*

at fourteen and finished her performance she ran out of the theatre in Mantua, Italy, ran through the streets, her soul filled with the persona of Juliet.

The beginning of Julie's conscious awareness of acting as a craft was in high school. She was always cast in the best parts in the Drama Club plays. "We had a wonderful, beautiful young teacher, a graduate of Vassar, who put on plays like *The Importance of Being Earnest.*"

It wasn't until she went to the Perry Mansfield Theatre Work Shop in Steamboat Springs, Colorado, that she began to harness her instinct for make-believe. To prove her seriousness to her parents she won a work scholarship and waited on tables for part of the tuition.

Of those early lessons Julie said, "I really wanted to be a ballet dancer, but I didn't have the discipline that was necessary. As for acting, I was always imitating someone. If a boy took me out and said, 'You know, you remind me of Bette Davis,' I'd *be* Bette Davis. That's what I was striving for, this 'star quality.'"

Winston Churchill once said, "We are all worms, but I do believe that *I* am a glow worm." So did Julie.

Besides movie stars like Ginger Rogers and Bette Davis, who were her youthful idols? Julie admired Helen Hayes and the Lunts. Her voice deepened with excitement when she mentioned them. "Suddenly Lynn Fontanne and Alfred Lunt would do something and I'd just dissolve. In *There Should Be No Night,* the scene when they were parting from their son; when he turned around, just in that turning I was gone, I was just gone, with the agony of it."

The essential part of Julie's training began at Yale Drama School after graduation from high school. That was when she started learning the techniques of acting, the first time she started to use her voice.

"I read Sarah Bernhardt's book about her memories as a young actress and she said she was terrified in the beginning because she didn't have adequate physical equipment; she would pitch the voice too high when it had to go even higher. But, having to do a play eight times a week develops your technique. You think, 'Where can I pitch my voice so it doesn't hurt?' That comes from doing scales; I just sing the scales. I do it every day and that's the only way that power comes. You know, after twenty years of touring and playing, eventually I learned something. I finally can act and think about my voice at the same time."

It is absolutely essential for an actress to be aware of what is going on, even at peak intensity. She must have total belief and control over all the elements of her performance. During those early years on Broadway, Julie was developing that important sixth sense without which an actress cannot grow.

I asked Julie just what "belief" means to her, and she explained it as being a "sort of *power* of belief, a willingness to immerse oneself in the subject, whatever it is." She mentioned a book about the Second World War, about the liberation of Auschwitz, that she was reading when she was in the process of filming a movie called *The Hiding Place*. "I began to cry and shudder and I wanted to go out and say to everybody, 'Remember this, think of this. This is part of our history, part of our lifetime.' I have a great ability to be caught up in something, in a story, and absolutely believe, believe I'm there. I want to give it to everybody and I want everybody to be concerned, as I am."

While still at Yale, in 1945, she was cast in the Broadway play *It's a Gift*. "That director said, 'When you say that line give a little flourish with your hands; raise your head up, chin up, when you say that line.' I said, 'I can't,' and I guess they thought, 'She can't do it.' I would try but my soul just began collapsing. I had my own sense of what I could and what I couldn't do, and I couldn't superimpose anything on it. It was a question of truth."

"The paper comes in a blue envelope and says 'Your services are terminated.' I thought, 'Terminated, what does that mean?' Terminated means ended. It couldn't be. 'What does that mean?' They said, 'You're fired.' I said, 'Oh, my God.' So I went to my friend's apartment where I was staying and the playwright, who was the leading actor, phoned me and said, 'Don't leave the city, we'll settle this.' I was rehired two days later."

The basic art of acting demands, in Shakespeare's words, to "force your soul to your own conceit." You are your own artistic instrument. You are playing on yourself as you would a piano or a violin. You use the same breath and body and soul that you use in real life, you must feel that what you are feeling, you are doing for the first time.

I asked Julie if, after such strenuous identification with a part, she was able to leave it at the stage door. She replied, "Eight performances a week are terribly demanding and hardly ever come up to my expectations. I was unhappy about it for years and years and years. It took me twenty years before I really knew what I was doing, so that I could slide into a part, use whatever energy and feeling I had, and work with that, not pump it up and demand too much of myself. It took years to be accepting of myself."

Senses work unconsciously for an actor, but they do not work if one is too set upon catching the thought. There are exercises performed while using ordinary objects. Julie's favorite exercise was holding an old tea towel with red and white checks and spots on it. Of that towel, which was connected to an emotional event, she said, "I had the old tea towel with the ink spots in my hand and then my emotions started . . ."

I commented on her remarkable voice, expressive as a fine-tuned lute. Julie said, "At the beginning, I couldn't use it consciously. I had to make myself forget all about it and just get on with the acting. Reality, truth, memory. I learned these things by osmosis, at The Actors Studio. I was a terribly slow learner and it took me years, but slowly I absorbed all that knowledge, excitement . . ."

Julie patted Teresa and continued talking, after a moment of drifting away. "I believe there is a pattern that your own personal energy creates, a pattern that you have to believe in and follow, but there's a lot of luck in the theatre and you've got to struggle to be as good as your luck."

Julie looked away again in an absentminded way. She said, her voice an introspective whisper, "Rita, for years and years I was fortunate in that I had beautiful parts to play."

She went straight from acting the barefoot twelve-year-old tomboy in Carson McCullers's *The Member of the Wedding* to play the restless young English wanton in the 1951 hit *I Am a Camera*. Her name went above the title of those plays and her acclaim grew with each succeeding production.

Shirley Booth said, "A producer can put your name in lights, but only the public can make you a star." Julie became a star not only to the producers of *I Am a Camera* but to the public as well after that first triumphant opening night.

Great acting is about a lot of things. Julie learned that from Ethel Waters in *The Member of the Wedding*. "Ethel Waters spoke about faith; she said, 'You have to have faith.' When I would say, 'Oh, God, I was so awful,' she would say, 'No you aren't, baby,' and I'd say, 'Oh, I get so frightened that I am not going to be able to do it,' and she would say, 'You've got to have faith, Julie, you've

Julie Harris in The Member of the Wedding *(1949). Courtesy of Julie Harris.*

got to start with that, you've got to have faith that it's going to be all right.' But it took me a long time to learn that lesson." Ethel meant that it would just *happen* on stage, to trust, to have faith.

Artistic results come from life itself, to create a moment of truth onstage. That's what Julie's acting is all about.

Harold Clurman directed her in *The Member of the Wedding*, and her sensitive portrayal of F. Jasmine Addams, who discovers the universal need of being "we instead of me," made her the shining new star of the 1950 Broadway season.

Julie talked enthusiastically about that rehearsal period. "Harold was a great one for inspiring you with 'Just go, jump, do it.' His direction reminds me of a very dear friend who talks and talks and talks and then you pounce on him and you say, 'Don't talk any more, let's just do it.' Harold was like that. He talked and the words just tumbled out and ideas tumbled out, you were immersed in his inspiration.

"After the second or third day of rehearsal, I said, 'Oh, Harold, I can't wait to do it, to try to do what you're talking about.' At the end of the first act, the 'we of me' speech, I was having difficulty in rehearsal—I didn't have any technique to do it. I didn't know how to reproduce it and I said, 'I'm having awful trouble with that speech.' He said, 'It's like a prayer. Just say it very quietly, like a prayer.' That was it. So simple."

Taking a breath, Julie said, "I had a tendency to overdo everything. Once during the 'man-oh-boy speech' when I was too hysterical, before Ethel Waters sings her song, I say, 'I'll go all over the world and when they get married they'll take me with them and we'll visit this place and that place.' I was sitting in Ethel's lap at the time; I just wasn't in control of it. At the end of the speech she caught me because I was hysterical but I was too theatrical.

"Harold said, 'I want you to do that speech with your arms down at your side.' And immediately I did it, I got down to the simple part of it."

Julie's eyes sparkled. "It was like you could never make a mistake with Harold. He gave you the feeling he wanted you to play. Oh, well, you know it was like falling into Heaven. He was such a gifted director and compassionate human being."

The very first step you take in creating a character can very often make the difference between a superficial performance and a creation of lasting depth. We talked about the different ways actors have when they start creating a character. Julie mentioned the production of Shaw's *Saint Joan* that Uta Hagen staged with Gladys Cooper's son playing the Dauphin. "I remember hearing about his performance at the Actors Studio. They said with reluctant admiration, 'Well, he works from the outside in, *but* he's very gifted. He does all the outward things of what costume to wear, "what am I going to look like," etc.'" Julie said, "I thought, 'But *I* work that way too.' I put on the clothes, I put on the shoes, and suddenly something starts to happen. Yes, it's like a little girl dressing up. It's almost like Mother's paper dolls. I say, 'Well, what kind of shoes would she wear, how would she cut her hair, would she wear perfume, would she not?' I begin to build a character that way. That's what I do, it's from the outside.

"Those outside things give me my feelings, and the character. The minute I see a color or fabric or gloves or shoes it makes me feel a certain way. Color and texture. . . . I knew the minute I had the dress, the high-heeled shoes, and the black stockings, and cigarette holder, and my green fingernails, I had that Sally Bowles. All of that gave me the character in *I Am a Camera*.

"In *And Miss Reardon Drinks a Little*, Anna Reardon was having a nervous breakdown. When in rehearsal, I found an old silk dressing gown that I had worn a long time ago and I wore that, not caring that my hair was not combed and I had no makeup on; then I suddenly felt right having a nervous breakdown. Those things, I am sure that's what does help me, start my motor going. There's the little girl in the attic saying, 'Oh, look at me now, I am this grand lady or I am Cinderella, or whatever.'"

Julie related her favorite story about Dame Wendy Hiller, who always asked herself in times of doubt or a crisis, "What would Sybil do?"—Sybil being Dame Sybil Thorndike, the compelling English tragedienne. In more than any other profession, actresses feel a kinship with one another, learn from one another, are fed by one another's triumphs and learn from their defeats.

Certain personal qualities helped Julie establish herself on Broadway: sensitivity, delicacy, intelligence; but it wasn't until Van Druten's version of *I Am a Camera* that the extent of her talent became evident. The madcap character of Sally Bowles called for an extroverted statement that was comedic in its thrust, tragic at the base. Julie had to become sexual and glamorous, enough so to manipulate several men.

"With comedy it's always a matter of finding the right proportions. You have to experiment.

"I was immediately categorized in *The Member of the Wedding* as a flat-chested and odd-looking girl," she told me," but when *I Am a Camera* came up she was bound and determined to be sexy. "John Van Druten read Cloris Leachman and every actress in New York for the part and thought he really wanted the English actress Joan Greenwood. When nothing worked, they decided to use me. I was lucky.

"*I Am a Camera* was larger than life and on opening night it was triumph, but I was holding back; it was in my nature. I was not satisfied with what I was doing. I was a fraud to myself."

Again, that theme from childhood, self-doubt, desire to satisfy, striving for perfection, on the opening night of her second great triumph.

An actor uses everything in the world to create: his experience, his sensations, his own flesh and blood. That, and the words of the author, to project his art. Unconsciously, or consciously, Julie's sensitivity and strength led her to her many great performances.

That age-old question, how does she go about learning the lines?

Julie answers, "If it is a long part I learn it before rehearsals start. For Emily Dickinson I had to learn seventy-five pages before rehearsals. I had someone come twice a week for about two months to test me. Studying for hours every day for eight weeks, raging, cueing, adjusting, digesting those works. You've got to chew them and chew them and chew them. I'd go to sleep not knowing them and miraculously wake up having them. You have to have the lines down pat to have the freedom to rehearse the play."

She smiled a sunburst smile and said, "Yes, it's like being a musician, knowing the score. It frees you. Instead of me taking the play over I allow *it* to pull *me* along. I think acting should be discovery. You go through all those rehearsals then throw everything out the window and rediscover it all over again with an audience. Their energy gives you the answers."

In 1976 *The Belle of Amherst* brought her her fifth Tony. "I identified so strongly with that part. I read a lot of her biographies and when I read one of her poems at a benefit at the Booth Theatre in New York, director Charles Nelson Reilly said, 'My God, that's exciting!' and we started that eight-year journey to bring Emily to life on the stage." Julie looked deep within herself to find that communication with Emily. About Emily, she said with a girlish intonation underneath her husky voice, "She wasn't morbid, she speaks to the lonely part of all our natures."

I asked, "What do you think of just before you start a scene?" Julie answered, "I don't think of anything. I start on that moment like Charlotte Brontë's words, "Sometimes the wind is so wild, unremitting, sweeping." Those words give me comfort and they sort of wash around me, and then my mind sort of goes into that groove of where she is. I'm really listening to the wind. Then I rest; it's like a mantra. It's as if I rest in the words."

Goethe said that an actor's career develops in public, but an actor's art develops only in private. Somehow, in spite of Julie's statement that she was only happy when there was a plan to follow, she has always managed to create her own plan. She looks deep within herself to find that communication with her character and then with her audience. About Emily Dickinson she said, "When I was playing her, she was always with me during the course of the day, always part of my mind.

"I start with my own self, my body, my way of speaking, and just work from there." All those things that we recognize as human on stage, actors create from themselves. But Julie, with her special

Julie Harris as Emily Dickinson in The Belle of Amherst *at the Longacre Theatre, New York (1976). Courtesy of Julie Harris.*

gifts of voice and sensitivity, has given us unique human portraits. As Jean Anouilh said in his play *The Lark* (a play Julie did to great acclaim), "We have made a lark into a giant bird who will travel the skies of the world long after our names will be forgotten or confused or shot down."

And Julie said very simply, her sturdy hands resting on Teresa's tiny sleeping body, "My ultimate satisfaction as an actress is doing it right."

I can only add, in Anouilh's words, "I hear distant music for her love for all of us . . ."

Glenda Jackson

It was noon and the workaday traffic noise of London almost drowned out Glenda Jackson's strong voice. Someone once said that she wore her face like the pale battlefield of class warfare, but the first impression I had was that her face was of a woman-child who promised everything. She could also have been centuries old, but it was a childlike sexuality that colored her fast-moving thoughts. Most evident was the stamp of the elitist artist, her keen intelligence.

Glenda was born in Hoylake, a small town near Liverpool. She was the oldest of four sisters. Her father, a jobbing builder in the navy, saw her only once in five years. It was during the war and all the men were away. Her mother, aunt, and paternal grandmother were the main influences in her life. Glenda said in a level voice, eyes looking back in time, "I was never really unhappy or in want, but it *was* hard to make ends meet. I can remember having a soldier doll that my mother made for me out of khaki and a Scottish doll dressed in tartan and velvet. When I showed the doll to my grandmother I dropped it and her face smashed to smithereens. I never wanted to think about that doll again."

The closest she came to acting in her English bread-and-butter childhood was playing the part of the little crippled boy in the Christmas play in Sunday School. "A star is in the sky," she said. Those words heralded the end of her brief acting career as a child. Soon afterward, she said wryly, she gave up religion, too.

Glenda Jackson as Hedda Gabler in TV-film Hedda *(1975).*

During a particularly rebellious adolescence she "curried favor" with her peers by hiding in a classroom cupboard and making mysterious noises much to the distress of her schoolmistress and happily to the amusement of her school chums. She blamed that on her hormones "going mad." She studied ballet until she became too tall to consider seriously a professional dancing career.

Her voice rising above the morning traffic, Glenda said, "I can't be precise about hindsight influences, but I do remember admiring actresses who weren't particularly glamorous in the traditional way but had strong personalities—Katharine Hepburn, Bette Davis, and Barbara Stanwyck played parts they may not have chosen to play, but they brought to them their own special view of the world. Theirs was an ironic view, and they made a very special place for themselves in the world."

What were her childhood ambitions? "I wanted to be a Wren but I gave it up when I discovered that I got seasick just crossing the local river. When I thought of nursing I found that I loathed hypodermic needles. Then I got a job as a salesgirl in a Boots Chemists shop. They disagreed with my ambitions to be the first female director of the company. I was fired."

Glenda paused and said, "Fortunately, a friend saw me act at a local 'Y' and encouraged me to go into the theatrical profession. She was the kind of friend that usually shows up in the biography of an actress." Pausing again, Glenda in her self-effacing manner said that the only drama school she ever heard of was The Royal Academy of Dramatic Art, where she went on to win a scholarship and grant.

She remembered John Fernwood, the director of the Royal Academy, saying to the students in his opening address that "theatre wasn't a glamorous profession but instead required discipline and hard work." That appealed to her own obsessive sense of discipline, and, true to her working-class background, she applied lifelong habits of hard work to her studies, all of which would eventually equal inspiration.

Remembering that her voice teacher said that she must have come from a very large family because she had a very loud voice, Glenda gave a soul-touching laugh that came from her toes and rose in waves to her childlike crew haircut. She said she spent a great deal of time eradicating her northern vowels and the flatness of her tone. By studying fencing and dancing she learned to respect her body as "the envelope of her soul through which the intention of the playwright would be channeled."

Glenda had a stripped-for-action look, and her multicolored vest, covering a well-toned body, was the only bit of color in an otherwise utilitarian drab outfit. She took on an aura of beauty when she relaxed.

As she sipped cold coffee from a styrofoam cup she said, "Learning the classics was a matter of course. Shakespeare is an integral part of the English tradition; his word was all until the fifties. Then ordinary voices began to be heard for the first time. An angry young playwright, John Osborne, burst onto the theatrical scene. A whole new range of attitudes grew up around the antihero. Actors finally stopped standing around on stage being admired for their looks alone." Glenda added that she was finally cast in parts for which she was right. "It may not have been much to go on, but it was a beginning, and I knew that there would be room for me in the newly emerging theatre."

Glenda auditioned for Peter Brook, who found her anger and energy just right. Peter Brook's theatre demanded all kinds of exercises and theatre games in training his creative core of actors. Among them they exploded tired old theatrical dicta. The group broke traditions and new ground with their improvisations, new sounds, and freer gestures and movements. Tied-up and tired English emotions finally exploded in truth. Glenda said, with excitement breaking into her multileveled voice, "I became part of a stimulating new theatre after years of being in the desert of the provinces. It was an oasis."

The group was soon adopted by The Royal Shakespeare Company, and Glenda went under contract to them for the part of the insane and murderous Charlotte Corday in *Marat/Sade*. With that grotesque and exciting production, the public persona of Glenda Jackson began to emerge.

When Laurence Olivier was the director of England's National Theatre, he admitted to an intense wish to make the audience watch the action with as much enthusiasm and fascination as they would watch a soccer match. Peter Brook did just that with *Marat/Sade,* where actors sat onstage at random in the original German production. Actors were characterless and only occasionally drummed themselves into some kind of general mob activity. In Peter Brook's production, every actor found individual characteristics; regardless of the size of the part, every actor worked on his part as though it were the lead. Glenda's Charlotte Corday was a nymphomaniac who went into a state of narcosis and violence. She felt that her madness was a kind of divinity. Ultimately, however, Glenda "got stuffed to the teeth with the repetitious nature of insanity," and found that to be mad was to narrow one's range of experience, not expand it as she had first believed.

Glenda was one of the first British actresses to take her clothes off. What could have been thought of as a "nude scene" just for the sake of shock in *Marat/Sade,* became, in her imaginative hands, riveting drama. In Ken Russell's film of D. H. Lawrence's *Women in Love,* "my nudity was essential and creative." Glenda said with grave composure, "I don't strip as a general rule, but sex is such an integral part of D. H. Lawrence that you can't be true to him unless you do it. I was pregnant at the time and had most beautiful breasts because all that milk was ready to flow." She continued with the seriousness of a biology teacher, "In Ken Russell's *Music Lovers* I was flat-chested again, but that didn't worry me. There are a lot of flat-chested people in the world. Anyway, I took my clothes off for intellectual reasons."

Fluency, flexibility, and technical precision are Glenda's gifts of technical mastery. She has carried her accomplishments to perfection on both film and stage. But she feels that the stage is more vital. On stage the audience is always a factor in your performance; in film you have to do a scene over and over again, without an audience. Ultimately you are unable to control the result. On stage you can figure it out, do it, and it's over. It has the excitement of a high dive into your emotions, very exciting . . .

Beneath Glenda's suburban exterior there are a deep sense of justice and a probing mind. Perhaps the secret of her talent lies in her complete acceptance of herself. She is free from false modesty, and her stoicism is deeply ingrained. She refuses to use theatrical tricks or clichés and has a unique ability to expose what is behind the human facade. These are the attributes of greatness. But most of all, her galvanic inner self shines through a thoroughly trained body and a psychologically free mind.

Her nerve, her guts, her sense of danger, make her great. But it is her honesty that sets her apart from "the usual" well-trained Brit-

Glenda Jackson as Gudrun with Jennie Linden as Ursula in film version of Women in Love *(1969).*

ish actress. She interpreted D. H. Lawrence without liking his philosophy, giving even greater dimension than Lawrence intended for his bitch goddess Gudrun in *Women in Love.*

Glenda remembered her performance with relish. "Gudrun, for all her pretentions and self-deception, had in her a genuine acknowledgment of that which is mysterious in life—not secretive, but genuinely mysterious. That gave her validity; without that she would be a petty, trendy pseudoartistic bitch." Glenda personified the free-spirited and antisentimental forerunner of the liberated woman. She emits a kind of honesty that could be construed as either inspiring or withering. But she is always courageous, like her or not. In the fifties Glenda came to personify the female psyche of our times.

With self-effacing modesty, Glenda continued, "It's been such a surprise to me that I have been given any work at all." Although she loved working with Ken Russell in *Women in Love,* he was furious when she turned down the part of the sex-starved nun in his next film, *The Devils.* She wanted a change of pace after playing Tchaikovsky's neurotic wife in his *Music Lovers.* Vanessa Redgrave played the part with great success. Glenda shifted gears and turned her intelligence and wit to comedies like *A Touch of Class* with George Segal, for which she won her second Oscar (her first was for *Woman in Love*). *House Calls* and *Hopscotch* with Walter Matthau were extensions of her comic vehicles. Bette Davis, Katharine Hepburn, and Glenda all have that golden statue in common, and a string of memorable liberated women who have broken through the dead ground of convention.

"I've never wanted to play any particular part, but there are parts I would like to play again. I'd like to play Masha again in *Three Sisters,* and Cleopatra. If I could stifle my actor's superstition, I'd like to have a crack at Lady Macbeth and, if someone could come up with workable texts, I'd like to do some of the Greek plays."

Taking a fresh breath, Glenda continued, "There are a few more Ibsen plays I'd like to explore. I found working on *Hedda Gabler* fascinating. We used a literal translation of the original Norwegian which I found was an extremely spare language with very few adjectives. The characters have a limited range of expression, they repeat themselves constantly, and they sit around and discuss life endlessly. They behave like a literary debating society with words and the expression of emotions. Through their words are the be-all and end-all of life. I've always wondered why I found them rather dull—interesting but dull—but they're not dull at all. They are absolutely meticulous pictures of what it's like to live in a small town in a country that is dark and cold and . . . and it's marvelous. And all that black, black humor . . . zinging through."

Glenda has become a symbol of a new kind of female sensibility. She is hard-minded and opposed to everything that is soft or phony in life. After a moment of silence over the steady droning of cars, she said with intensity, "When a woman gets over the forty hump she has a lot to say. There should be parts that make demands on the experiences she's gained by living. But they just aren't there as they are for men."

Had acting become easier for her? I asked.

"The more you do, the harder it becomes," she insisted. She was harder than ever on herself and hard on each performance she gave. She said: "Actors should leave their egos outside the theatre."

I wanted to know where else she wanted her career to go. Had she considered directing?

Personal photo of Glenda Jackson. By courtesy of Glenda Jackson.

Glenda studied the coffee container for a moment; she seemed to be listening to a distant drummer. "Yes, I'd like to direct someday, if, as a woman, I'm given the chances. I don't see why women shouldn't be extremely effective as directors. We have an instinct for relationships and emotions and we have the practical ability for simple staging. A woman makes an environment for other people to live in. We can make that happen on stage and film as well as in a private house." She continued, her enthusiasm growing, "Yes, more than stage, I would like to direct films. Directors create the atmosphere for the bricks and mortar to be made. Then those bricks and mortar are directed into a house. But we have to be given the opportunity to do it."

Regardless of how many films Glenda has made, her feeling about the theatre remains the same, and she hasn't allowed dust to accumulate on her Chekhov, Shakespeare, and Shaw. When an audience accepts their responsibility, really good performances occur. "The actor is the channel through which the author speaks, and the circles of thought and energy that go from the stage to the audience and back again are the actor's responsibility," she said. "Even so, the audience has to do more than just buy a ticket; they have to be open to hear and see and reinforce the actor with their receptivity." She said that she has played audiences where she had to tell them what to do. "They mustn't be too eager and yet you have to tell them where and when to come forward and when to wait. Should they want to be onstage with you, you have to let them know when to get off stage and push them away if necessary."

Peter Hall once said in an interview about Glenda, "You cannot look at this woman without feeling you've matured five years at least." I can see how one could feel distanced by her single-minded intensity, but I can also see how the British institution of "Our Glenda" arose. They recognize in her the sister, mother, wife, they always dreamed of having. Within her spunky raw delivery they recognize their own verifiable honesty. They find in her the new English liberated woman.

So does the world.

Maureen Stapleton

"Wow, I cheated death one more time," said Maureen Stapleton, eyes wide with the drama of her statement, face mobile and expressing love. That's how one of America's finest stage actresses feels about acting on stage.

Mo, as her friends call her, came from Troy, the small city in upstate New York. She has a strong Irish Catholic background, and her view of life is one of the uneasy observer. From the age of six onward she went to the local movie house every day after school and stayed until closing time. She wanted desperately to be part of that world where "everyone was so pretty and seemed to be having such a good time." She said she loved Jean Harlow and thought that if she became an actress she'd automatically look like her. Her voice lowering, eyes even wider and somehow startled, she said, "That's how I got into the rat race."

Her parents were separated when she was five. She and her mother went to live with her aunts. She was a dreamy, unhappy child who spent her early years surrounded almost entirely by women, with the exception of an adored absent uncle.

Mo burst onto the Broadway scene in the early fifties when the wheel of fashion turned away from the nineteenth-century star vehicle to plays of frustration and neuroticism by a passionate Tennessee Williams. Her lusty sensitivity was a perfect foil for Williams's comic-tragic heroine in *The Rose Tattoo*.

The part of Serafina had been written for the great Italian actress Anna Magnani, but she was afraid to act on stage in a strange language. Critic Kenneth Tynan wrote that "the part of the Sicilian firebrand was the most thoroughgoing star vehicle in the past ten years." Mo filled the bill. She understood from the top of her head to the tips of her toes the nervous power, the brooding hysteria of the Williams heroine. The *New York Times* said, "Maureen Stapleton's performance is a triumph. The widow is unlearned and superstitious and becomes something of a harridan after her husband dies. Miss Stapleton does not evade the coarseness of the part. But neither does she miss its exaltation. For Mr. Williams has sprinkled a little stardust over the widow's shoulders and Miss Stapleton has kept the part sparkling through all the fury and tumult of the emotion."

In the 1950s psychoanalysis was often the topic of the day on the cocktail circuit, and neurosis the badge of artistic greatness. Mo, with her multitudinous phobias, made good copy. When asked what she was afraid of, she answered, "I hate high buildings, I hate airplanes, I sleep with a pair of scissors under my pillow, I hate trains and cars; it's kind of tough for me to get through the day." She won public favor with her emotional warmth and unsentimental wisdom. A fickle audience was appreciative of her self-effacing charm that turned eccentricity into folksy humor.

Edith Evans, the duenna of the British theatre, once said, "You really only begin to act when you leave off trying." That quality of "not trying" is the signature of Maureen's talent. She is realer than real, more honest than life.

Acting for Maureen is intensely personal. One accepts an occasional cliché because of the depth of her emotion . . . it startles. In a confidential tone, one octave lower than her vulnerable middle register, she relates how in one of her first Broadway plays, *The Bird Cage,* she played an alcoholic woman. "Although my father had been an alcoholic, at that time I knew very little about the craving for alcohol. I substituted a craving for candy, chocolate, my secret sin, the shame of being addicted to sweets, my secret vice. It's all the same thing. At that time I didn't know what it was like to be a drinker." She paused and with an ironic look added, "God, I know now . . ."

Once between a matinee and evening performance of *The Rose Tattoo* she went to a cocktail party and had a lot to drink. It was a

Maureen Stapleton in Tennessee Williams' The Glass Menagerie *(1965), Brooks Atkinson Theatre, New York. Courtesy of the Springer Collection/Bettmann Archive.*

nightmare—not only for her but for the other actors. "It scared me so," she confessed. "Crazy thing to do. I got through the play by the grace of God, but I swore to myself that I would never, never drink before a performance. Never risk it. It was a false relaxation, a false prop, and it doesn't work. George Scott later told me that that experience probably saved my life."

Stanislavsky considered theatre to be a religion, a temple where actors were priests laboring for their God. He created The Method as a guideline for the training of actors. Although Mo first thought of acting as a road to riches, a way of "being swathed in furs," all that changed when she started studying in earnest as an advocate of The Method, which she discusses in the codified vocabulary of theory and in her own brand of street talk. She translates it into practice, giving force and meaning to technique. There is truth in the saying that "actors are born, not made," but Mo's encounter with The Method provided her with a special and reliable highway by which her talent could progress with surety, a way to illuminate parts with consistency, poetic insight, and humanity.

She said, like a child proud of being part of a grown-up game, "If there's something wrong in rehearsal, like if you're having problems with your pipes, you call a plumber, he'll fix them for you. The same goes for acting, if something is wrong and if your director has common sense and intelligence, he can fix it for you, and perhaps contribute an interpretation that is richer than your original concept."

She considers laughing very much more difficult than crying. She said, "If you have leaky ducts like me, crying is a cinch. But laughter, which in children is a free, beautiful emotion, on stage appears to be just a nervous reaction. It has to be practiced until you can do it automatically." She told how Marlon Brando taught her the secret that Oscar Homolka taught him—and then demonstrated it by letting all her breath out of her body and saying "HA HA HA" and building up to a crescendo by pumping more and more air into her lungs until she achieved a real laugh.

I tried pumping air and saying "HA HA HA" along with her and we both sat laughing and crying with the effort.

Mo refers to The Method as all that "inner stuff," but she practices it thoroughly. To be true, to be real, to keep the part alive, are objectives of the system, but she was first taught the Delsarte System by Frances Robinson Duff, her first drama teacher, who was an exponent of that outmoded system where the body was divided into spheres; the hands and eyes and eyeballs expressed the strongest emotions, the other areas of the body assumed prescribed positions for every emotion from rage to love. Mo lifted her eyes to the ceiling in mock horror and laughed—a deep raw ironic laugh—as she told me that she didn't understand a word that Frances Robinson Duff said.

She continued her early studies at the Herbert Berghof Studio and took night classes at the New School for Social Research while working at penny jobs during the day to support herself. She learned to "live" on stage by The Method: the spine being the mainspring of building a part, actions and beats being the way of arriving at it. She learned the importance of listening, and the purpose of her character in relation to the others in a play.

Mo thinks of acting as a "job"; she goes to the theatre just as other people go to work from nine to five. The moment she arrives at the theatre she starts to prepare for her "work" on stage. Part of the job is to be heard in the balcony. She considers her naturally strong voice a tool. Once she gets a part she sticks to it to the letter, keeping it fresh by strictly following the notes of the stage manager.

Mo thinks of herself as "a slow learner," and a character develops at its own pace in rehearsal. She spoke about "that awful day when the director says, 'Don't act,'— which means it's time to really act your ass off. Some things come more easily than others, and that's the moment when everything falls apart and you have to go back, taking a little step at a time. Acting is like charting a ship's course; there's a certain distance you have to go, and you've got to steer the course using just the amount of fuel you need."

Lee Strasberg once said that the ability to be private in public was the most difficult task in acting. In real life Mo is unable to cope with practically everything in her immediate environment, but on stage she has the uncanny ability to take an audience into the deepest reaches of her heart. She releases emotion with startling abandonment, never externalizing her inner intentions.

Although considered one of the greatest exponents of a Method actress as practiced by the Actors Studio, she makes fun of their excesses. In an interview, she related how when Noel Coward went to the studio one day he said, "What is going on here?" Mo said, "Oh, Noel, it's fun, it's nice here—it keeps me off the streets."

Maureen Stapleton and Elia Kazan. Photo: Rita Katz.

And he replied, "You belong on the streets, and the next time Lee Strasberg asks you what you were working for, say—money."

Mo's quality of erotic despair was perfect for Williams's prototype of the strong woman who becomes the heroine-victim at the hands of society. In the fifties, if a woman followed her sexual instincts, she suffered for it. In his *Battle of Angels,* Williams told that tale of pain and unrepressed emotion. It was an early play that had opened in Boston in 1940 and closed immediately after receiving disastrous reviews. He rewrote it, calling it *Orpheus Descending,* having Mo in mind to play the embittered Italian wife befriending an itinerant youth who wanders into the violent atmosphere of a small town in Mississippi. Thomas Nash said Williams had "written a stinging and passionate saga of terror, injustice and bigotry, and Harold Clurman directed it with a superb sense of spiraling crescendo of taut suspense and tumultuous emotion. Maureen Stapleton illumes the total effect with one of the most moving and powerful portrayals of the entire season." She created a character with whom the audience could safely entertain sympathy and yet could feel compassion—a woman of that time, volatile, tough, vulnerable, and lost.

An actor's edict is that it takes twenty years to make an actor. Such is not the case with Maureen Stapleton. Mo's talent unfolded with immediate force, and Broadway's trendy acclaim kept her waiting for worthy vehicles for her talents.

In 1970 Neil Simon came through with a play that erased the line between life and art. He wrote what was considered a bleak but sometimes clever comedy called *The Gingerbread Lady*. It was the struggle about "a woman who drinks"—a battered, manic-depressive divorcée who barely gets through the world. She fights for her life with a barb and a freewheeling wisecrack. Clive Barnes, then critic for The *New York Times,* said, "Maureen Stapleton is quite wonderful, the baritone note of outrage in her voice, the friendly despair of her manner, the fierce anxiety, yet even fiercer pride, of her attitude, all combine in a portrait of a memorable lady. Childlike, innocent, confused, sly but trusting—Miss Stapleton plays her game of solitaire with no card unturned."

Was that a bit of theatrical voyeurism? The Method says, do what the character would do in the situation, but I suspect Mo's own life was used as an example, her senses evoked. In the part of Evy Meara, the boundary between technique and life was nonexistent. Mo's own brashness and her frightened plea for help were the bones and flesh of this haunting performance. As English actors are wont to say, "She had the character under her skin." Mo made the character have contact with the real world with a defensive joke only a second after she leaves that world. One senses a void that is filled in life only by her children. All else is chillingly uncomfortable and unreal.

Mo's concentration is what keeps her grounded. She said, "Whatever I do has to be total. If my mind is on the shopping list, kazoo, the show is over. Even if I just sit there and listen, really listen, or put my concentration on a pillow, or another person, or a prop, nobody may notice anything but that focus is what brings my concentration back into the scene. Each object is life-giving."

Sir Desmond MacCarthy, the English critic, once wrote, "The summit of the actor's art is to make us forget that he is an actor. Only then do we share intimately the experience of the creator's characters." If we use that critique for great acting, Maureen Stapleton is among the great. But like most professionals she is unaware of her power, unsure and always striving. Face glowing, she related an incident that occurred with actress Mildred Natwick. Mo asked her, "How does it feel to be a great actress?" Mildred looked at her as if she was insane. Mo thought, "If *she* doesn't know, then *nobody* knows." When I asked the same question of Mo, *she* looked at me as if I was insane, and I thought if *she* doesn't know, then *nobody* knows . . .

Appearance and reality, shadow against shadow . . .

Our interview was over and I took Mo into the hallway. She closed her eyes and took my hand when she got into the elevator and said she was afraid of heights; she hated elevators and mechanical things of all kinds and wished for a simpler age.

Zoe Caldwell

Zoe Caldwell is the kind of actress who alchemizes the air around her. Her intensity is so infectious that one finds oneself listening to the simplest story as if it was earth-shakingly important. Her jokes seem funnier than other people's and her descriptions, more vivid. One feels more vibrant because of her presence. In life as well as on stage, Zoe has a sense of drama as large as the country she hails from, Australia.

She was born in 1933 during the worst of the Depression; her father, an unemployed plumber, worked as a bouncer at a ballroom where her mother was a dance hostess: an inauspicious beginning for this intensely gifted actress.

Zoe recounted her conception with lusty enthusiasm. "I think it's awfully good to feed children some marvelous story about their conception and birth and all that stuff; even if it's a little untrue, it's jolly nice for a child to know 'their' story. It gives them something good. My mother told me that the owner of the ballroom, Percy Silk, owned a tiny house by the sea in Chelsea and she and Dad went down there for the weekend and I was conceived. Everyone said, 'You can't afford another baby, for God's sake; you can't afford to feed three of you now. Get rid of it.' But Mum didn't and I was born, and it turned out just swell. I slept in Mum and Dad's room till I was seven. Mum and Dad loved each other. It was a very good nurturing time. They were real mates."

She continued in her highly colored voice. "As a child I had motor skills disability. I was unable to distinguish my left from right, but very early on I realized that I could sing, and dance, and move. I was good at imitations. They sent me to dancing class when I was two; and I was onto my first concert at two years and ten months."

For about ten years Zoe studied tap and ballet and a form of eurythmic dancing and was taught diaphragmatic breathing. From the age of seven she studied voice. Because of a learning disability, she was taught to sing in "a very sweet voice" and to dance. "In that I could express myself," she said, "but I couldn't do anything like math. My mother had been a dancer before her marriage. She had toured Europe, India, and China."

Had Zoe been influenced early by *her* dreams?

Peter Brook once said, "An actor is someone who allows the truth to pass through them for a moment." Zoe's acting not only allows the truth to pass through her but does it with such unique mastery that one could believe that her technique was instilled in the womb.

When I asked her about Stanislavsky's place in the development of her technique she replied passionately, "Good actors do what Stanislavsky says, but they do it of their own volition. We all of us come to acting from such different areas of life and emotions. The one need, somehow or other, is to communicate. When you're acting you feel potent; I don't mean because people are looking at you and clapping and asking for your autograph; I don't mean that kind of potency. That's peripheral nonsense. The real power is the power of being potent, feeling I am communicating these words and emotions to another human being."

She spoke of how the goal of most actors is to achieve that total mastery over themselves, not to "act," just to exist, "to be"— which takes an enormous amount of confidence. What she now realizes is that *that's* the very thing that really does entertain. A person can't take his eyes off a kitten or a child when one of them is completely lost in itself or completely absorbed by something else. We are all mesmerized by that, and that is the big thing with acting."

She continued, "Jessica Tandy does that in *Foxfire*, with a kind of being, just being." Her hand movements, graceful but definite, punctuated her sentences. "I think the English actor starts right from the text, specifically from what is written and 'grammatically' what is written. American actors are trained for the most part to fill a part emotionally; they are a bit fuzzier, but somehow deeper and more potent."

She has the ability to make an acerbic commentary about herself with the wit of people who work with their hands, under a sunrise-to-sunset sky. In her nimble voice she recounted a story the beloved director, Harold Clurman, told her when they were working together on Eugene O'Neill's *Long Day's Journey into Night*. It was about the great actor from the Yiddish theatre, Rudolph Schildkraut, watching the first performance of his son Joseph. "He sat in the back of the theatre. When Joseph came on stage wearing a very large, very black, false beard, Schildkraut said to himself, 'Beard, beard, where are you running with my son?' Zoe, when I watch you act I want to get up and shout, "Characterization, characterization, where are you running with my actress?"

Zoe continued, "I understood, I just understood inside. Harold made me stand still. Instead of moving around the stage and doing a lot of stuff, I did absolutely nothing, I mean nothing. Well, suddenly there was a great welling forth of emotion that I'd clearly kept trapped by working so hard at entertaining. It all came spilling forth and I had the most extraordinary acting experience."

She paused for a moment, then continued, "To do nothing on stage is very difficult for me. Usually I feel my responsibility to entertain the troops, to give people their money's worth, keep people awake and in their seats. If I sense the audience is getting restless I'll keep the ball in the air, I'll move in all over the play just to keep them in their seats."

She sighed. "Sometimes I'm too much, too often."

The kinder side of Zoe's technique is found in this review by Robert Pasollini:

Miss Caldwell, a virtuoso character actress, has an extraordinary gift for vivid physical embodiment; like many classical actors, she pins her character to an imaginatively chosen and precisely articulated constellation of physical gestures, then proceeds to create a remarkable degree of full-life. Her initial statement of physical life is stunning, and the fullness of character she unfolds is eminently dramatic.

The goal of Miss Caldwell's technique is to establish a ruling tension in her characterization. She brings it about by laying down the character's area of constraint, and then by finding the character's mode of vio-

lating the constraint. As Frosine in The Miser, *her robust, conniving spirit would flash up from the company manners she assumed as a guest in the miser's home; as Natasha in* The Three Sisters, *her predatory urgency would fly up from the social and spiritual inferiority to her sisters-in-law; replacing Anne Bancroft as the Prioress in* The Devils, *her maniacal obsessions would surge up from the tight decorum of her behavior as a cloistered nun.*

The drama of Miss Caldwell's performance as Jean Brodie resides in a tension which she creates in this fashion.

Zoe Caldwell as Helena with Dame Edith Evans in All's Well That Ends Well, *Stratford-on-Avon (1959). Personal collection of Zoe Caldwell.*

Zoe is always open; she is always searching for ways to make a performance deeper, truer, more explosively real. She uses all means at hand and she can be ruthless in her research. When she played Colette in 1970 she went to France and visited the places where Colette lived, spoke with Colette's husband and daughter, and with the tradespeople who had known her. In the course of her research she discovered that her own grandfather had come from the Mauritius Islands, as had Collete's father. Everything became threads that sewed the part to her own skin.

The *Wall Street Journal*'s review said about her portrayal of Colette:

Miss Caldwell is quite simply mesmerizing, giving one of those flamboyant performances that prompts thoughts of legendary actresses of the past. With hair like a large abandoned bird's-nest, a body teetering between the voluptuous and the dumpy, a throaty voice that never quite suppresses the growl at the heart of the cooing, she thrusts herself about the stage like one of Colette's favorite cats, lazily, almost ungainly, but always insidiously and seductively. There are the rolling consonants ("I'm powdering myself. I must make myself presentable.") and the flirting vowels. ("I have never lost the habit of maaaarveling.") There are the deliciously eccentric clothes and the defensively vampish posturings. There is, in short, an unforgettable performance.

Her creation not only has great emotional impact but also makes a personal statement. Zoe's portrayal of Sarah Bernhardt was remarkable in its specific and meticulous detail.

Initially Zoe wasn't interested in playing the Divine Sarah. Then she read everything written about her. "I didn't care about her," Zoe said in a conspiratorial tone of voice, "until I came to where she slept in a coffin. I began to understand her and get inside her skin."

Zoe explained in vivid detail how when Sarah was fourteen she was told she was dying of tuberculosis, and she said to herself, "Well, if I have only six months to live, I'd better stop wasting my time looking over my shoulder and being afraid. I'd better make friends with death." That's where the coffin came in. It was really a very practical thing, not just hocus-pocus. She persuaded her mother to have a coffin made and lined with perfumed pink-rose satin. She kept it in her bedroom and would take a nap in it every afternoon instead of on her chaise.

Sarah also had a human skull that she put her hands around and held affectionately. It was like holding a sphere. It was soothing. She had made friends with death, and having done so, she went on to live a long life without fear, filling her life with outrageous acts. "Wasn't that marvelous?" Zoe asked, as she ended her story on the tail end of a long breath.

Zoe chooses to play worthwhile and infinitely complex women, from the Divine Sarah to Lillian Hellman. She not only interprets her ladies, she inhabits them.

Of *Medea,* directed by her husband, Robert Whitehead, she said, "I wanted to make her really foreign. When I read myths about her it seemed to me she was beyond knowing. I wanted to make her like someone you don't understand and are not sure you want to. She'd come to Corinth, a pagan from a society where the prime goddess, the goddess of the earth, was a woman. Everything about her was foreign, truly foreign. When one reads about horrendous acts of butchery in the newspaper and it stirs something in you, it makes you afraid, repels you, but you can't stop reading about it. Even as you fear, a primal thing is sleeping inside your fear. I wanted Medea to do that to people, so ultimately they could understand her murders."

Zoe was fascinated by Medea's sexuality. Her theories, firmly nailed to reality, were as impassioned and exalted. They were extensions of what is workable and true. "I felt that with ladies like Medea and Cleopatra," she said, "sexuality was much more prevalent."

Medea's nurse, as the caretaker of royalty, would allow Medea to do anything, even masturbate if it calmed her down. Dame Judith Anderson, who played Medea originally and triumphed in the part in 1948, understood that. . . . Zoe's and Judith's experience seemed to coincide as they both had interpreted Medea as a primitive, possessed woman, a witch.

"What was extraordinary this time around was that the connection we had on stage was really rare; it was as though Judith and I were actual extensions of one another."

Zoe's life always had an element of fate about it. When she was supposed to enter the United States to play the scheming matchmaker in *The Miser* and Natasha in *Three Sisters* for Sir Tyrone Guthrie and the Minnesota Theatre Company, permission was refused because she was not considered a star by American Actors Equity. Fortunately, when Zoe came across the border to Minnesota from Canada, she was admitted to the United States by an immigration officer in Saint Paul who had never heard of Actors Equity.

Her success in *The Miser* was immediate. Walter Kerr said in his *New York Times* review, "Zoe Caldwell is spectacularly good as a thoroughly unreliable matchmaker, wrapping her voice around Hume Cronyn like the wings of a dishonest angel."

Zoe had this to say about working with Guthrie: "I was Tony's pet, and when he got bored in rehearsal he brought me in for laughs. He put me on stage to keep everyone's adrenalin up and keep the other actors' energy from slipping. I had the facility to stand on my head and bounce two balls with my feet, and do all that lovely stuff that keeps the audience awake. He encouraged everyone else to do really marvelous and true things, and with me it was a hands-off policy except when *he* wanted to be amused."

Fate intervened again when Zoe was understudying Anne Bancroft in *The Devils* on Broadway. Zoe was at my house having dinner when the stage manager rang to tell her that Anne Bancroft had hurt her back and Zoe was to get to the theatre immediately and take over for her in the second act.

Without a second's hesitation she collected her coat and purse and stuffed my makeup into her pocket and took a ten-minute taxi ride from Park Avenue and Eighty-ninth Street to Broadway and fame. Her performance in the last two acts of *The Devils* is now theatre legend.

Zoe is quick and passionate, like some more-than-human creature; during the course of a conversation she remains attentive, eyebrows arched, her face as motionless as a print. She exudes an assurance that seems to be a legacy from her frontier background.

In private life, Zoe is married to producer Robert Whitehead—and she possesses three Tonys and The Order of the British Empire. "Mateship" is what she calls her splendid marriage with Whitehead, an elegant Canadian and first cousin to Hume Cronyn; he produced both *The Prime of Miss Jean Brodie* and *Colette* for Zoe. When they married, in Bucks County, Zoe was decked in lilac and with fresh lilies of the valley in her hair. The local postman and his wife were in attendance. Zoe says of her life: "I am of the theatre and I'll be playing parts till I won't be able to remember words, but the windfall of my life is Robert and the boys"—Sam and Charlie. "They have made life extraordinarily rich."

Zoe Caldwell in the title role of The Prime of Miss Jean Brodie *(1968).*
Personal collection of Zoe Caldwell.

Zoe feels that directing is the logical next step for her. That is an extension of acting. Her first effort was *The Taming of the Shrew* for the American Shakespeare Festival.

With compelling accuracy her husband, Robert Whitehead, directed her as Lillian Hellman. But it is Zoe's own otherworldly talent for transmuting her heart and soul into that of another that brings audiences to their feet. They behave in that same way in which the nineteenth-century audiences were reported to have acted, with extravagant bravos and cheers. . . .

There is mystery in Zoe's talent; in her incarnations, greatness. Grinning a devilish grin Zoe explains that "Zoe" is the Greek word for life, and says in her sweetest voice, "The theatre is my life and always will be . . ."

Actors Studio Originals:
Viveca Lindfors and Geraldine
Page

The only consistency that the leading actresses of the Actors Studio have is their lack of consistency in acting styles. They are as different as the months of the year.

I particularly admire Estelle Parsons, with her streak of New England eccentricity, and Ellen Burstyn, with emotions like an unbridled forest fire. And of course there was Marilyn Monroe, America's most treasured film goddess, whose blond luminosity shielded her Anna Christie from the slings and arrows of a cruel world. I have acted several times with Viveca Lindfors, but it was Geraldine Page who has captured my imagination the most.

Viveca and I were first together in David Susskind's spirited TV version of Thornton Wilder's philosophical novel *The Bridge of San Luis Rey*. Versatile, electric—she is the quintessential actress. Swedish by birth, American by adoption, a most faithful exponent of the Stanislavsky system, she is original, brilliant, and egocentric. She does strange things on and off stage. Sometimes I had the feeling that Viveca thinks in Swedish and translates as she goes along, but often she can be profoundly accurate in her emotional choices.

She graduated from the Royal Dramatic Theatre in Sweden and was brought to the United States by Warner Brothers. She starred in more than fifty films, but it wasn't until she abdicated her Hollywood throne and portrayed Anastasia on Broadway, in her own vivid, true way, that she really came into her own.

Viveca is a beautiful woman who can act. She was extraordi-

Viveca Lindfors in Nicholas Ray's King of Kings *(1961). Personal collection of Rita Gam.*

nary in her solo portrayal of thirty-six women in her one-woman show, *I Am a Woman*. Intricate and balanced, she brought to life Shaw, Ibsen, Colette, Shakespeare, Sylvia Plath, Brecht, and a battery of emerging women's liberation writers.

I remember her best from a time we shared on a sun-baked location in Spain, during the filming of *King of Kings*. Head thrown back, hands moving with dramatic emphasis, back arched gracefully, a husky laugh—she expanded on the theory that Jesus Christ was really an angry young man.

Viveca, looking very much like a Viking goddess on the prow of a sailing ship, began practicing her castanets, to the consternation of the sound crew. One Sunday, in the middle of our long shooting schedule, she invited the cast of international stars to her country house for a smorgasbord lunch. The table groaned with dozens of cold delicacies, and as I was accepting a sandwich from Hurd Hatfield, a horse appeared at my elbow. "Viveca," I called, "Viveca, there's a horse at the table." Viveca called back, "Vel, vay not? A horse can be hungry, too."

We worked together again in 1961 in the Actors Studio goodwill tour of South America in Tennessee Williams's *Suddenly, Last*

Viveca Lindfors (1983). Photo: Rita Katz.

Summer, Edward Albee's *Zoo Story,* John Van Druten's *I Am a Camera,* and Strindberg's *Miss Julie.* We presented the five plays in three evening cycles in Buenos Aires, Mexico City, Montevideo, São Paulo, and Rio de Janeiro.

We started out with an ideal. "Everyone must vote on everything and everone gets equal billing" said fair-minded Viveca. "We are a very democratic troupe."

It didn't work out like that when we landed in Argentina. Viveca, in miles of mohair, gave interviews that earned headlines such as LA VIVECA AND HER TROUPE ARRIVES. But all through South America she tried to be fair, and we took turns using the nineteenth-century dressing rooms of great actresses like Eleonora Duse and Sarah Bernhardt. They were filled with the memories of triumphs past and ghosts of the great. Viveca would lie flat on the dressing-room floor and I would stand on my head to relax before our performances. The spirits of actresses past swirled around us, no doubt giving weight to our "Method" performances.

Shortly after the opening of *Suddenly, Last Summer,* our friendship began to cool. Viveca took to puffing on the cigarette that my character, Cathie, dropped on stage, and she painted a mustache on her upper lip to characterize her part of the nun. I felt the audience's laughter wasn't quite appropriate for Williams's Gothic tragedy and made my feelings known. We just made it through the opening of *I Am a Camera,* probably because of the high we all felt from being part of a successful venture.

The South American audiences loved us. The intensity of "Method" acting, and wonderful actors Betty Field, and William Daniels, and Ben Piazza's deep-felt honesty thrilled them. The audiences came to the theatre expecting a dose of decadent American culture and found only all the problems of their own lives—drunkenness, incest, drugs, prostitution, and homosexuality. They gave us a standing ovation on our last curtain call and I began to worry, as the mob surged toward us at the back door. As we raced into the alley next to the theatre, we thought that the revolution the State Department had warned us about had begun. All this delirious ebullience was only the South American way of saying "We love you."

By the time we got to filming Jean-Paul Sartre's *No Exit* in the primitive film studio on the outskirts of Buenos Aires, we were so cold that even the badly heated barrels of fire that were used to keep

Viveca Lindfors and Rita Gam in a film version of No Exit *(1962). Personal collection of Rita Gam.*

us warm failed. I remember filming a rather delicate scene between the nymphomaniac Estelle (me) and the Lesbian (Viveca). The scene called for Viveca to try to kiss me. Viveca was astounding in the part, different and brilliant, but when she kissed me with rape-sized passion and forced her tongue down my throat, she took me by surprise.

Perhaps I overreacted by spitting, but I wasn't ready for quite that much reality. Nevertheless, the moment was effective enough to electrify audiences and win the Berlin Best Actress Award for both of us. I attended that year's great international film festival and picked up the silver Berlin Bear for best actress, along with one for Viveca. The bears made my luggage overweight, but I lugged them to New York and handed Viveca hers with a hug and a big kiss.

It was a typical blustery March day when I visited Geraldine Page in her tiny dressing room in the Music Box Theatre. I had spent a happy year in that very same dressing room in the British hit farce *There's a Girl in My Soup*. Gig Young and I had a glittering time cavorting through sexual innuendos with a fine British cast, including Jon Pertwee, Gawn Grainger, and Barbara Ferris.

Gerry apologized for the smallness of the room in her "voice of feathers," as she once described it. "We should have done the interview on the Brooklyn subway, going to my son's class day."

"This is fine," I replied, settling into a familiar chair.

There were pictures of her children and postcards from friends from around the world lining the walls of the room. She was removing the knee pads that she wore as the nun in *Agnes of God* and taking off her makeup. Her dresser was measuring her for the costume that she was going to repair for the evening performance.

Geraldine Page and Lee Richardson in Tennessee Williams's Summer and Smoke *(1952), Circle in the Square Theatre.*

After having seen her in *Summer and Smoke* and *Sweet Bird of Youth,* I found her acting marked by a rare sensibility, and I was looking for clues as to how she arrived at some of her results. But, like many fine actresses, she is unable to explain how she acts.

I had watched Gerry work at the Actor's Studio, and I am reminded of the time when Peter Ustinov, the distinguished and funny actor, whispered to me, after having watched Gerry squirm through an hour of Lee Strasberg's nonstop criticism, "Won't someone please get the poor girl a lawyer?"

Gerry's openness on stage and off might be one of the components of her talent, but Harold Clurman said of her in Richard Nash's sentimental comedy *The Rainmaker,* "She does an amazing quantity of external things; she hops, flutters, and runs throughout as the spinsterish Lizzie and even plucks and bangs and fiddles with shoelaces, but her entirely original rhythm weaves an odd but frequently fascinating design."

Gerry says she is the kind of actress who leaves her character at the stage door. Though she has won several Academy Award nominations, the Donatello Award, two Golden Globe awards, and two Drama Critics awards, one Sarah Siddons and one British Academy Award, personally Gerry is a most unassuming woman. But I found it difficult to penetrate her midwestern stolidness and down-home modesty. It is impossible to sit in the same room with Gerry and not feel admiration for her qualities of vulnerability. One wishes to protect her from a humdrum world that might harm her.

Gerry looks older than her middle years. She almost prides herself on her negligence, but she became beautiful as the fading movie star in *Sweet Bird of Youth.* She transformed her own slight frame and nervous gestures into a portrait of this Williams heroine that was unforgettable.

It is in the film *The Trip to Bountiful* that her raw sensitivity and homey looks make the heroine Carrie Watts, who wants only to return to her Texas birthplace once before she dies, into a triumph of naturalness. Gerry's is a performance of such spontaneity that she gives new meaning to the word "acting." After eight nominations, Gerry finally won the coveted Oscar for this performance.

"She can't say hello without its being an event," said Gerry about the Princess Pazmezola in *Sweet Bird of Youth.* She credits that transformation to director Elia Kazan who, when she was working on the part, told her to play the part with "splash." He handed her an album of portraits of famous movie queens Mary Pickford, Pola Negri, Clara Bow. It was a portrait of Norma Talmage that gave her the clue that she was after.

She is versatile and astonishing. She is quiet and unassertive about her effects and then when you aren't looking she moves in a way that catches your breath and suddenly reveals the soul of the character she is playing. As the nun in *Agnes of God,* at the end of the first act, with body taut, face pleading, she turned her back on the audience and extended her arm in a way that was heartbreakingly revealing. She acts with her entire body. Her hands are almost never still but every movement has meaning. When she is at her most concentrated, she can be magnificent; at her worst, she flutters but somehow remains interesting.

More than beauty, she possesses the rare ability to listen to other actors on stage and live truthfully under imaginary circumstances. Her inner rhythm is always in proportion to the emotion, and she seems to radiate warmth and light and credibility.

Gerry said of acting in comedy that she "loves the freedom it gives her on stage." She has more than a sense of comedy. I believe that Gerry, in the pure sense of the word, is one of the few lady clowns in the theatre (along with Carol Burnett and Nancy Walker). As she stretched her ever-moving body and her rubber mask face in the Mirror Repertory Company's production of *The Madwoman of Chaillot* and Booth Tarkington's *Clarence,* she reached the outer limits of clowning.

"Boy, if it's this easy, I want to do this forever," Gerry said when she was eight, noting the tears rolling down the cheeks of her audience in church.

She dreamed of being a concert pianist, but her father, an overworked Chicago doctor, couldn't afford the piano. As a youthful amateur, she played every part she could get. When she wasn't sweeping the stage of a little community church theatre, she was acting.

After checking hats in nightclubs, modeling lingerie, and wrapping spools of thread in a factory, Gerry became a theatre star at a time when being a star was primarily privileged to the film industry. TV and movies now created the stars, not the theatre. But Gerry attained stardom in the traditional way with her first three Broadway plays, and was one of the last great talents to do so.

"It was fun seeing my name in lights for the first time and after it was painted on posters in subways. I liked to stand out there and let them blink right back at me. I don't think being called a star has changed me much; outside of acting, there are four important things in my life: husband (actor Rip Torn), food, children (we move as a troop), and alarm clocks . . ." she said, with her voice trailing off into her usual vague silence.

I heard a voice calling somewhere in the theatre, "Miss Page, Miss Page." Her voice trailing off into whispiness, Gerry seemed to swallow her thoughts as she let these words fade away too. "It's so

Geraldine Page (1984). Photo: Rita Katz.

wonderful when people tell me I look divine in a part. I don't care if they even mention my acting . . ."

There was a knock on the dressing room door and a young woman stood shyly with toes turned inward and stammered that she would like an autograph for her collection.

Gerry's face beamed with pleasure as she excused herself to write her signature.

Joanne Woodward

Walking gingerly through the wine-bottle-strewn streets of Soho, I thought how ironic to be playing the smallish part of Paulina in Chekhov's *The Sea Gull* while Joanne Woodward would play the pivotal part of Madame Arkadina, the part every actress of certain years longs to play, a part I had played with great satisfaction a few years back. Yet I was delighted for the opportunity to watch Joanne build her character from scratch. "Yes," I told myself fatuously as I walked two steps at a time up the steep stairway to our rehearsal loft, "There are no small parts, just small actors."

I have known Joanne ever since the golden years of television when I was married to Sidney Lumet and before Joanne was married to superstar Paul Newman—in fact, before he made his film debut.

I was immediately charmed by her fiftyish good looks. Her hair was ash blonde and sometimes white in the light. Her skin radiated health from a sensible diet, and her body was slim, small boned, and almost athletic. She was bursting with inner-and outer-directed energy and she was knitting away at the longest, peachest sweater I had ever seen. I was to see a lot of that sweater. She worked on it until opening night at the Byrdcliffe Theatre in Woodstock, when it was miraculously finished, and replaced by some blue tweed wool.

Joanne was chatting away with our talented director, Larry Sacharow of the River Arts Theatre, and our young cast. It was obvious that she was enjoying the camaraderie of the first day of rehearsal. Joanne said, "Working on Chekhov is like peeling an artichoke. It takes time to get down to the heart of it, what's really going on. There's a kind of life underneath that I don't think you find in other playwrights. That's what rehearsal explorations are for, to find it, and it's a bitch."

I remembered this well from my own wrestling with Madame Arkadina's soul in Syracuse. Joanne was attempting the transformation of an American film star of middle years to Madame Arkadina, a mid-nineteenth-century Russian actress of the "grand" temperament. It wouldn't be easy.

There was enormous drive in Joanne's approach to the part. Much of it is creative energy and some of it nervous energy. The first reading was interesting in that Joanne didn't *push* for characterization. Her first reading was like a parked car with the motor on, but going slowly. Throughout rehearsals her character began to emerge. There was logic in her choices. They were brave and true choices. She was not afraid to find the qualities in herself of spitefulness and envy. She didn't feel obligated to win the audience. She worked on the body language of the character, an aspect of the characterization that she feels keeps her on the right track.

The difficulty of this role is that Madame Arkadina is neither the direct cause nor the principal object of the play's action, and the power and success of the role depend to a large extent on what the actress brings to it in revelation of passion, vanity, endearment and cruelty, tenderness and self-absorption. Quite a challenge!

After several weeks of talk, exploration, improvisation, and soul searching, a subtle, complex, and always believable Madame Arkadina began to emerge. Always contained, Joanne moved and looked like a Toulouse-Lautrec poster, in a shawl and a period corset on the outside of her rehearsal skirt. She never left anything to chance. She was meticulously specific, a quality she mentioned admiring in Laurence Olivier when she did a TV show with him.

Joanne mused on the wisdom of knitting in the play. She asked, "It was done in that period and Arkadina would have the habit of knitting backstage, wouldn't she?" That was one of several free associations about choices she would make. She did a lot with props; an endless supply of "things" seemed to appear magically from the depths of a blue carpet bag. There were constant activities that were consistant with her "mother earth image." I was curious

Joanne Woodward (1986). Photo: Rita Katz.

as to how many would actually find their way into scenes in the play.

Joanne thought quickly and aloud a great deal of the time. That aspect of her personality grew with sure effectiveness into quick-witted and abrupt changes of emotion on stage. She captured the warmth, the charm, and the sexiness of the aging provincial Russian star, without sacrificing pettiness and her fear of growing old, which, of course, is at the core of the character.

It was lovely to see the layers grow day by day in that dim loft.

"My acting teacher, Sandy Meisner, used to tell me," said Joanne, "that you have to learn to be an actor the way you learn to play a violin. The moment finally comes when you're playing the violin and you don't have to think about where to put your fingers. The same thing should happen to an actor. There's a moment you don't have to say to yourself, 'What is my motivation for this scene? Where am I going and what am I doing?' That is when you have it."

I admired the surety of her method of work. She slowly found the character within herself, summoning precisely the right sensations, dipping into her memory bank of experience, doing only what related to her and the character. Hers was a fine example of Method acting.

Joanne said, "Acting is rather like stringing a bead necklace. Each bead you put on is a moment, and when you act it's moment to moment." Joanne never actually set a scene completely—a lot was left to chance. "Whatever feels right, I do," she said. "Whatever clicks. Without that, one's bag of tricks gets used up so quickly."

When Larry Sacharow staged the poignant seduction scene between Arkadina and her younger lover, Trigorin, which was played with brilliance and insight by actor/writer and Pulitzer Prize-winner, Michael Cristofer, they never firmly set anything and the impulses of the moment led invariably to hilarious improvised hysteria. It was as far out and funny a scene as I have yet to see in Chekhov. With fierce sexuality and laughter she pinned Trigorin to the couch and seduced him with the surety of a Feydeau heroine. When she played with Deidre O'Connell, a marvelous young actress, one of the loveliest and most original Ninas I have seen, Joanne knew her own patterns of behavior so well that she could trust her instinct of being jealous and could take what came from Deidre and fly with it. That kind of acting takes courage, and confidence, and it gave color and fluidity to the familiar text.

Joanne's career has been very special. She is an Oscar-winning actress who actually preferred television to feature films. Her first feature film was on loan-out to Columbia, *Count Three and Pray* with Van Heflin. But she emerged as a star when she undertook the demanding multiple role in Nunnally Johnson's production of *The Three Faces of Eve*. She was named in all the critical polls as having given the best performance of the year, received the National Board of Reviews accolade of "Best Actress of the Year," and topped it all off with an Oscar for "Best Actress" in 1957.

Joanne continued as a star of major calibre, playing a wide variety of roles in films such as: *The Long Hot Summer, From the Terrace, A Fine Madness, WUSA, Winning, Summer Wishes, Winter Dreams,* and *Harry and Son,* among others. Versatility has been her criterion in choosing scripts. She loves roles that are a challenge to her ability, and diversity has been the presiding theme throughout her career.

Her range of offbeat portrayals has given Joanne's career depth, although she never actually found that niche that secures stardom on a flamboyant level. Perhaps because of the variety of women she portrayed, she never really formed an "image" with which a public could identify.

Working in television now, she finds, "is a lot less tedious than features and the finished product is seen by millions of people almost immediately, giving one a very quick reaction to your work." Her TV films have included "Passions," with Lindsay Wagner and Richard Crenna on CBS, "Crisis at Central High," "The Shadow Box" by Michael Cristofer, "The Streets of Los Angeles," and "See How She Runs." Her most recent Emmy triumph was "Do You Remember Love?" co-starring Richard Kiley. It was a realistic study of Alzheimer's disease.

Joanne's favorite film director, not surprisingly, is husband Paul Newman.

She starred in the screen version of the Pulitzer Prize-winning play, *The Effect of Gamma Rays . . . on Man-in-the-Moon Marigolds;* it was directed by Paul. Her previous collaboration with him in *Rachel, Rachel* resulted in an Oscar nomination. Newman won the New York Film Critics Award for his direction of the film. "He has such perception. He always knows the overall intention of a scene and he doesn't talk me to death. He just finds a word," Joanne said, with more than a little pride and a lot of love in her voice.

Her work is perhaps best exemplified by the fact that the last six television films in which she has starred have won a total of five Emmy nominations and one Emmy, not to mention her twelve fine films and an Oscar for *The Three Faces of Eve.*

"I was born wanting to be an actress," Joanne told me. "My first appearance was when I was two. It was with my brother, who was five years old and very shy, and we were supposed to recite the Pledge of Allegiance. When he got sick, I went on for him and recited it to thunderous applause. I came back and did a third and fourth rendition. They couldn't get me off the stage. After that the die was cast. I was an actress for life." Catching a breath, she continued, "My mother was a cross between Janet Gaynor and Billie Burke, but she lived in the South at a time when becoming an actress wasn't done. I came along just in time for the Shirley Temple curls, and in time to carry out all her aspirations."

When we shared a rustic dressing room at Byrdcliffe and spent that rather special hour transforming ourselves into Chekhov women, Joanne into the glamorous Arkadina and me into the lovesick Paulina, we dodged mosquitoes and communicated in whispers.

I wanted to ask Joanne about the things one doesn't usually talk about in a shared dressing room. That time is devoted to deep communion with one's soul and doing voice exercises; and strangely enough, the only things we talked about with each other were banalities like face-lifts, hair sprays, children, and old boyfriends—girl talk. So the Sunday morning after *The Sea Gull* opened and we were a smash, Joanne and I decided to discuss acting problems of mutual interest over coffee.

I know it sounds like a busman's holiday, but it was mighty pleasant to sit on top of a Woodstock mountain terrace and drink coffee while the windchimes were gently tinkling in the background—and "dish" about acting.

"When I finally get before an audience and I really find out what's going on in my character's head," said Joanne, sipping her coffee, "my comfort comes from knowing moment to moment what the other character is thinking." She took a Chekhovian pause and continued, "My concentration is never the same in rehearsal as when I am on stage. I get it from the other actors, from listening and knowing who, what, and where I am and what I am going to do."

She is not strong on theory. "Acting is like sex," she said. "You should do it, not talk about it."

Joanne Woodward as Madame Arcadine, rehearsing with Michael Cristopher for the River Arts Repertory's production of Chekhov's The Seagull *(1985).*

Her Madame Arkadina was notable for the many emotions she found in the character, the "different colors." She changed the part somewhat, added to it, made me long to see what the next actress who plays it will discover.

Joanne's was a lovely presence as Arkadina, she was the quintessential actress. When I saw Paul Newman before a performance, I said, "Wait till you see Joanne's Madame Arkadina." He looked straight into my soul with those earth-turning blue eyes and said: "Yeah, I know. She'll knock your socks off."

Part Three
THE CLASSICAL TEMPER

Wendy Hiller

I was in no mood to interview Dame Wendy Hiller. It was raining and I had jet lag *and* I was more than a little frightened. "She takes being a Dame very seriously!" I had been warned. On the telephone she *had* seemed all business, though quite courteous. I should be brief, I decided. To the point.

The combination of jet lag and worrying and planning had made the hour from London to Beaconsfield vanish. Suddenly, I was there.

It was still raining—it would rain that whole afternoon—but here the air seemed more invigorating. My jet lag was resolving itself and I could focus on the glorious-though-damp countryside. Everything seemed graygreen or graybrown—not drab, really, but muted. In the first moments of clear thought I had almost forgotten my mission when—blam!—I caught sight of an empress in tweed skirt and the reddest—or so it seemed among the country colors— sweater I had ever seen.

"My dear, how nice to see you! Isn't this rain a pity? Are you wet? I wish I had thought to bring an umbrella. How was the train?"

Any fears I had about this Dame were gone.

We got into her shiny green Austin and zipped through long alleys of elm trees, chatting about this and that, not really getting to anything like an *interview*.

She stopped the sedan in front of her home. Brick, 1914-ish. Sensible. And, like her sweater, red.

Wendy Hiller in Waters of the Moon. *Personal collection of Wendy Hiller.*

"Ronald is in the garden, working."

As she seated me in her cozy living room I became aware of the most wonderful sweetness in the air.

"Beech cherry. Isn't it a nice fire? Would you like tea?"

I said I would, and settled down to work.

Listening to the tea-making noises in the kitchen, I set up my tape recorder and went over a few notes. The room was so comforting—seductive, almost, that I kept losing my train of thought. Idly, I would glance at a picture on the end table, wonder how Ronald was making out among the soggy impatiens, or guess about some knickknack or other. Suddenly the door flung open and out marched Dame Wendy without benefit of tea trolley, tray held high.

"I can barely boil an egg or add up, but I do make a nice pot of tea!"

Almost before I had my cup in hand, her glorious mezzo-soprano was recalling the past—her happy childhood in Cheshire when her father was a mill owner.

"I was never beautiful, never beautiful at all. Plain, and skinny. It's very strange, that . . . I learned to sew and play the piano, but I could never cook."

I asked about her beautiful voice.

"I was very lucky. For some reason I had what was known as an elocution mistress. My father, who was German, was rather sympathetic to my going on stage."

She smiled conspiratorially.

"I must have inherited his stubbornness."

She sipped her tea and remembered.

"You see, my mother was most enthusiastic. She organized charades and children's plays and loved the *thing* of children acting. We played for them in old-fashioned candlelight."

I could see the fire reflected in her eyes.

"I was always a bit of a show-off, and nobody seemed particularly horrified when I said I wanted to act. I mean, I always *had,* you see. Even when I was tiny, my brother and I loved to play games—burial games, mind you! We walked about with a doll's pram, pretending that our teddy-bear rag dolls had died. We cried ourselves silly, tears streaming down our cheeks, our faces swollen with misery. Nanny was furious. We had a gorgeous time."

"So," I asked, "there was no opposition to your becoming an actress?"

Confusion crept across her face, quickly followed by surprise and then sly glee.

"I may have misled you, my dear. Have a brownie, and I'll explain."

I helped myself to a sticky piece of heaven.

"You see, nobody seemed horrified when I said I *wanted* to act, but when I actually came to go into the profession, Mother was dreadfully upset. A middle-class girl from the north of England? Fifty years ago? Well, it just wasn't done."

"What did you do?"

"I told you I was stubborn."

With a resounding clink, she deposited her cup in its saucer, rearranged herself on the overstuffed sofa, and outlined her attack.

"Since it wasn't quite respectable for a girl to live away from home at eighteen, I got a job as stage manager at a weekly repertory theatre near home. Manchester Repertory Theatre. Currently a *bingo parlor.*"

She pronounced the words with patent disgust.

"I swept floors and played small parts and rehearsed plays six days a week, fifteen hours a day. My feet were so swollen I wondered how I could keep my shoes on for opening night. Even so, they didn't think I was good enough. Sacked me. Then, two years later they were desperate enough to hire me back. Needed someone who could do a Lancashire dialect on short notice. I was happy they didn't ask me to sweep the stage as well."

The play was *Love on the Dole,* a comedy written by Ronald Gow and Walter Greenwood, about the Depression. The success launched her career and changed her life.

"We played it in London and New York, where I met the author and married him. He's the Ronald working in the garden right now!"

My thoughts turned again to damp Ronald, yet unseen. I pondered and mused as Dame Wendy's narrative turned to another remarkable man.

"George Bernard Shaw. They called me the perfect Shavian woman, but I wasn't quite sure how he would feel about it."

She refilled my cup and watched until I had a sip.

"I met him at one o'clock in the morning after a dress parade of *Saint Joan* at the Birmingham Repertory Theatre. Backstage. The theatre was filthy—no, not filthy, just *dusty*. I was fussing with a rather inadequate suit of armor, having just been abandoned by my dresser. I heard a voice and turned 'round and he was standing there and seemed to me to be surrounded by a blue light. He was tall and elegant and strong. So strong. He was big. Big, and he had a thin beard, red hair, reddish gray, and blue eyes. 'What's the matter with your hair, baby?' His voice was a wonderful, light tenor. 'I straightened it with bay rum and water,' I told him, 'but when I got under the lights—it frizzed.' He seemed to accept this. He spoke again. 'And what were you doing in that red dress?' Or did he say green dress? I can't remember, isn't that strange?"

Her voice trailed off into a whisper. I asked about *Pygmalion.*

"Oh, we became great friends over that. After only five rehearsals he said to me, 'You are playing your favorite tricks for all they are worth. I told you they would fail, and now I'll tell you why.' He never knocked you down without giving you the means to build yourself back up. I worked and worked, and after the dress rehearsal I summoned up the courage to ask him what he thought. As soon as he caught sight of me, before I could even ask, he boomed, 'My word! You're a whopper!' To this day it remains my most treasured compliment."

Wendy Hiller in Shaw's Pygmalion. *Personal collection of Wendy Hiller.*

Dame Wendy excused herself and went into the kitchen to get more brownies. When she returned, we talked about *My Fair Lady* and how ironic it was that Alan Jay Lerner turned the most anti-romantic comedy of the century into a classic Broadway musical.

"I've always wondered what G.B.S. would have thought. Probably would have laughed and said, 'Thank god for the money!' Oh, I don't know."

She got silent again and my thoughts returned to Ronald. I was formulating a most interesting theory when she announced:

"You know, he wrote Eliza for Mrs. Patrick Campbell. But

when they made the film she was a bit too old, and I was just the right age. G.B.S. wouldn't give permission to film it unless I played Eliza. I was awfully lucky. I couldn't go wrong with it as long as I waited at the right times. I never asked what the motivation was. I just paused at the commas, breathed at the semicolons, and swallowed at the full stops. Oh, and I never forgot to pronounce consonants. Do you know what I mean?"

I assured her that I did.

Things got very quiet suddenly. The fire continued to blaze and occasionally pop. I became aware of the ticking of a clock, but couldn't seem to locate it. Dame Wendy got a faraway look in her eye, as though consulting some mental filing cabinet, and I realized what intense energy was coursing through this wonder of a woman. She took up speaking so quickly that the sudden intrusion of her voice into the room startled me.

"Leslie Howard," she announced, "scared me to death. I couldn't bring myself to call him Leslie. He was a Big International Star at the time, you understand. That's why I surprised myself when, upon meeting him for the first time, all I could think was: Men are certainly getting smaller! I felt like a giantess. Oh, well, I thought, I'll just take my shoes off."

She chuckled benignly and paused again.

"Was he difficult to work with?" I asked.

"Well . . . I couldn't discuss anything with him. And I felt awkward. Tony Asquith directed it, and he's a darling. But the producer, old Gabby Pascal, wouldn't talk to me—just quarreled with me because I wouldn't sign a long-term contract. G.B.S. never set foot on the set, so he was no help.

"When we got to the tea-party scene, Mr. Howard insisted I play it one way. I wanted to shout, Look, I know how it works! But I was too frightened to talk and too stupid to argue with him. So I marched into my dressing room and wept bitter tears. Wilfrid Lawson came to me and said, 'Don't take any bloody notice of him, just get on with it.' It took two hours for the swelling to go down, and then I *just got on with it—my way!*

"Then of course, they saw the rushes, and I was everybody's marvel. Even Pascal started being civil. Of course he did—he realized what a good thing he had!"

Again she got pensive. I could imagine hearing the fireworks on the set.

"But in spite of it all," I said, "it was a wonderful film."

"I hated every minute of it," she said, softly.

I began groping about mentally for a quick change of subject. I settled on Sir Tyrone Guthrie, the founder of the Old Vic, and a director who had worked with both of us.

"When I worked with Tony Guthrie . . ." I began. Waited to see if she would take the lead. Silence. A log fell and I jumped a foot.

"Another one who scared me to death! I did a heavy season with him at the Old Vic—pure terror. I think what was so intimidating about the man was that vicar tone—but, really, there's never been a kinder or more generous human being.

"When I absolutely rebelled at playing Helen of Troy in *Troilus and Cressida,* he came to see me in my dressing room. 'Look,' I told him, 'I don't know how to work on Helen and I am exhausted and I want to leave the company.' I was shaking with fear. He looked straight into my eyes and said, 'Oh, yes . . . Helen. Rather old Clara Bow, a bit on the bottle, Marche Militaire on a white piano.' I felt as if someone had thrown cold water on my face, knew exactly what he meant, and got on with it."

I asked her about her favorite playwrights, and how she felt they stacked up against the modern ones.

"Oh, well, take Ibsen, for example. There is no more demanding writer than that man—I have a never-ending battle with him. You have to really hang onto the tail of those parts. I think the English never really capture that feeling of the far North, any more than Anglo-Saxons can ever play Celts. I don't think it matters as long as the whole cast share the same problems, and there are no real Scandinavians around. *John Gabriel Borkman,* for example, makes *Who's Afraid of Virginia Woolf?* look like Mrs. Tiggy-Winkle. Quite a challenge, indeed. But, I have a strain of the Northern people from my father's side of the family, so I have a little more understanding of those Ibsen ladies."

Indeed she does. When she was doing *When We Dead Awaken,* director Michael Elliott said she pursued the part with almost unbearable self-criticism. She seemed possessed of an overwhelming desire to do "the right thing."

"I wonder how dear Ronald is getting on. He *will* work in the garden, rain or no. I'll put on some more tea water. Sha'n't be a moment."

Again she was off to the kitchen. My legs were a bit stiff from all the sitting in planes, trains, and even this sweet armchair. I stood up and walked to the window. Tiny rivulets sped down the immaculate glass, struck the mullions, split, spilt over the edge and dripped downward. I tried to see the mysterious Ronald, but there was no sign of him. Dame Wendy seemed to speak always with one eye on me and the other on Ronald, wherever he was. I had almost finished the theory I had begun to formulate when she first spoke of him. Somehow I had the feeling Ronald was not in the garden. . . .

"There! Water's on. Where were we?"

"It's so peaceful here, I've almost forgotten." I murmured.

"Well, let's talk about *something*! Ask me a question," she suggested.

"How did you feel upon winning the Oscar for *Separate Tables*?"

"Good question, my dear."

I felt like the star pupil of a favorite teacher.

"When I won," she continued, "I thought it was incredible. Quite incredible. I was on the screen a short time, or so it seemed. All I seemed to do was walk in and out of doors and look over my shoulder at Burt Lancaster. My two best scenes were given to Rita *Hay*worth."

"The director got a psychiatrist to say that it was better for my character to give the scenes to Rita. But then, of course, Miss Hayworth was married to the producer. Convenient. She was a darling girl, though. Very shy. She always made me feel such a lump. Her bones were like a bird's—real dancer's bones."

I reminded her of what she said at the time she accepted the Oscar: "I hope this means hard cash, never mind the honor."

Dame Wendy smiled, sipped some tea, and stared at me.

"I meant it, too! Anyway, I like the theatre best. Movie cameras have always frightened me, and it's so exhausting to be always frightened."

The kettle started whistling. She got up and went back to the kitchen again.

I reflected on this dauntless woman while she busied herself with more tea preparation. She seemed at once a contented and a haunted person. Someone who has devoted herself to her art, and has asked nothing in return. And yet there is a bit of the shy, expectant schoolgirl who keeps waiting for a pat on the head that never

Wendy Hiller in Ibsen's John Gabriel Borkman. *Personal collection of Wendy Hiller.*

quite materializes. Certainly Dame Wendy Hiller has gotten her fair share of head-pats from the critics.

I remembered what the critic of the *Christian Science Monitor* wrote of her performance as Josie in O'Neill's *A Moon for the Misbegotten*.

She "becomes transformed from a sly humored sulking slattern into a woman of generous compassion and courageous dignity— O'Neill's symbol of the earth mother. Her speech is not foul mouthed, her tone does not rasp. As Josie, Miss Hiller triumphs over a somewhat incongruous accent to give a triumphant, full-scale performance of O'Neill's monumental heroine from a rural Connecticut slum."

Not bad for a woman who once said in an interview that she didn't take the theatre very seriously. She said she preferred gardening, and as she got older, she felt more and more absurd up there on the stage.

As this memory of gardening thrust itself into my thoughts, I found myself finishing my fantasy of Ronald, the mad gardener of Beaconsfield. I fancied him pruning saplings and fertilizing the soil, rain or no. But my other, tenderer theory about the mysterious missing husband was less colorful. I imagined him, frail and delicate, off in some upper room, resting in bed—Dame Wendy gallantly tending to his needs while the Visitor from America takes notes and drinks tea. My reverie was interrupted by the reentry of my hostess onto the scene.

"Do you know," she began, "I think I've talked myself into the ground. Why don't you join me in the kitchen—for some quiet."

I followed obediently.

After a quarter-hour of silent sipping and munching she related a final anecdote.

"I remember once in a rehearsal of something or other, I asked Sybil Thorndike—whom I knew all my working life—'Sybil, when will it get easier?' She looked at me as if I were a half-wit and said: 'It will only get worse, my darling. Naught for your comfort, my darling, naught for your comfort.' Do you know, it *does* get worse? Cruelly, nature takes confidence away instead of giving it!"

She stopped abruptly and shot me a shocked look, as though she had received and given the revelation in the same instant.

"All those years of experience," she went on, "and I've never really stopped unclenching my toes in those satin slippers."

Her words moved me deeply. I wondered about all the glory and triumph she had endured, never really enjoying or accepting it. I was about to get quite depressed when I looked up from my steaming cup and caught sight of the warm, Hiller smile. It disarmed the intensity of her confession.

I gathered my materials while the beech cherry fire, now a few glowing embers, discharged the last of its lovely radiance. I told her I was sorry not to have met Ronald, and asked her to give him my regards. She said she would and we slipped outside, made our way through the drizzle to the car, and drove back to the station.

"Please, don't get out," I begged, "I'll dash for the train. Really, it was so sweet of you to see me."

"Not at all. I enjoyed it—all that old business. Please keep in touch."

I assured her I would, and we said our good-byes.

I watched her drive off, until the little green car was just a spot against the misty English sky.

My train came, I boarded, found a seat, and settled in for the ride. Only this time I was not alone. I had journeyed to Beaconsfield in the company of a combination of jet lag, awe, and fear, but I returned to London at the side of the palpable memory of a "whopper" named Wendy.

Constance Cummings

Our next door neighbor in Church Street has a shallow pond about four by five feet full of goldfish. Several times we have seen a heron fishing there, and often when it is disturbed it flies up to the top of one of our trees in our garden and sits silhouetted against the sky for several minutes before flying away.

It is a rare and lovely sight to see in the heart of London.

Yours faithfully,
Constance Cummings
Chelsea SW3

It was the week before Christmas and King's Road was crowded with tourists from the Midlands, Scotland, and Wales. Loaded with brightly wrapped packages, they scurried in and out of the Peter Jones department store.

I was frantically looking for the location described in a letter to the *London Times* from the expatriated American stage star Constance Cummings.

Constance is a lovely example of reverse Lend-Lease. Having had, in her early years, a conventional success in Hollywood, in her later years her career blossomed into something nearly unique. An American actress, she became a great British theatre star.

She was awarded the Order of the British Empire by Queen Elizabeth. It is the second highest honor that a woman can receive in Great Britain.

I stepped into a crowded pottery shop and bought Ms. Cummings a ceramic butterfly for her Christmas tree and made inquiries as to how I could find her house on Church Street. The owner graciously explained that the numbers jump around out of sequence, but if I kept walking toward Brampton Road and looked closely the house would be on the right—I couldn't possibly miss it—.

I did just that, and like Alice in Wonderland I could not find heron or pond or any numbers. I was lost. I finally did come across some sort of a bird sitting on an odd-looking roof and, taking a chance, I rang the bell.

The critic's darling of two continents opened the door. A sunny lady, Constance Cummings ushered me into a Walter Gropius drawing room. The atmospere was reminiscent of the American West. Unexpected in tradition-bound London, comfortable, well-spaced contemporary furniture faced window sills lined with cactus plants straining for a touch of winter sunlight. Constance filled the room with a glow of her own, a glow of California light.

In her mid-seventies, still lovely with bright blue tropical eyes and chorus-girl legs, she spoke with a spunkiness that belied her years. There was not a vestige of musty memories or yellowing programs proclaiming past glories . . .

As a child growing up in a raw northeast Seattle, Washington, she was a self-proclaimed "goodie-goodie" who spent all her off-school hours studying to be a ballet dancer. "When I was seven," Cummings said as a flicker of childish disappointment passed over her face, "I was supposed to see Pavlova dance. This was going to be a wonderful thing. My God, I got appendicitis. It was terrible. I couldn't go and would never see her."

So vivid was her delivery as memories flooded her conversation that I could picture each moment clearly. She filled her words with vitality and immediacy. Then she talked about her mother, and the warmth of the woman's love filled the room. I was reminded of the tributes other actresses paid to their mothers' supportiveness, a recurrent theme I noted before in the lives of other actresses.

"My mother was a woman with a lot of zippity-do and go-go guts. She wasn't easily defeated. But she did rather have ideas about how nice ladies behaved," Cummings said with remembered joy. Her voice became contemplative as she continued. "My mother and father separated when I was fairly young, and my brother was

Constance Cummings in Glamour *(1934)*.

rather an iconoclastic little boy who was always getting into trouble. I always did what I was told and even went around picking up pins. . . . Mother always wanted a daughter, and we were very close and got along well."

"I'd thoroughly enjoy reaching the age of five hundred," she said. "I would spend part of my time acting the parts I haven't played, like Queen Elizabeth and Lady Macbeth, and part of the time studying astronomy . . ."

Constance worked for a lifetime, learning and relearning her craft. When I asked what she considered to be the single most important element in acting, she said without a moment of hesitation, "Concentration. That's it. It's so bloody difficult." Her voice rose with excitement, and I could feel intensity ignite her words. "I used to play a game at parties asking for a telegram that you most wanted to get. I remember one guest said, 'Am sending down gift of concentration. Signed, God.' True. True."

Constance talked about "energy," the most mysterious component of an actor's talent.

"I think energy, a good store of energy, is the real secret. Energy on stage is the real secret. Energy on stage is many things. In everyday life, energy makes us move with precision, whereas on stage, the more an actor uses excess energy and acts in a purely theatrical way, the more he blurs his objective and confuses his action. You create false notes when you overextend yourself." She spoke also of the energy one needed to get through a play. "When you are exhausted, it isn't any good if you play it as if you *are* exhausted. Yes, it takes a great deal of energy to 'do nothing' on stage."

As if demonstrating the demands of acting, she continued the discussion at a full non-stop high-energy pitch. "All this false mumbling, scratching, naturalist thing of acting. You don't behave the way on stage that you do in a drawing room. In a drawing room you aren't monitoring yourself. But on stage, every gesture you make has to be of use, just as in a well-written play, every word, every comma, has its place."

Constance's theatrical career began when she was a chorus girl tapping her way through lush Broadway musicals like Gertrude Lawrence's *Treasure Girl*.

In a non-auspicious Hollywood career in the 1930s she was always cast as the nice sister, the dull secretary, or somebody's daughter. Her lackluster career in the golden gristmill known as Hollywood ended after she failed to land a lead opposite Ronald Colman. This failed histrionic effort won her a one-way ticket back to tapping in Broadway musicals while her mother sold china in Wanamaker's department store. Her career leapt decisively forward when she married British playwright Benn W. Levy and came back to star on Broadway in his great comedy hit of the thirties, *Accent on Youth*. That was the beginning of a passionate, personal, and professional partnership. She has made her home in London since that fortuitous meeting.

"It was a marvelously satisfying marriage, and I'm still living it," she said, years after his death, with the adulation of someone deeply in love.

"By then, I was truly launched in the English theatre," she said. "It was not quite so enterprising as it is now, but over the past twenty years my roles have become deeper and deeper. I've always worked." In crisp British fashion Constance continued, "Now that Benn is gone I probably need more than ever that turn-on that acting gives."

After a hiatus during which she bore a son and daughter, Constance played with the Old Vic Company and in the West End in a succession of classics and hit plays. She has spent more than half a century on stage and screen making comebacks. But it wasn't until her discovery by London's theatrical elite that a fine career was constructed out of their desire to work with her.

"The theatre offers communication with the audience. You share something together. There's a subtle difference; in the films you know emotions are canned, so does an audience. The magic is missing," said the ever-enthusiastic Constance Cummings. By the note of wonder in her voice, she could have been an eighteen-year-old student at the Royal Academy of Dramatic Art.

"Take Rex Harrison, for example. He looks like such a natural actor," she continued in a stream of breath. "When he comes on stage it looks as if he does just what comes into his head, whereas he's really a most careful, meticulous worker."

Constance went to the kitchen and came back with some packaged toll-house cookies and instant coffee.

"I think you need something to hold onto onstage, don't you? We all do, or else you sort of float." Constance offered me a cookie and laughed at the memory of Sir John Gielgud rehearsing Pinter's *Homecoming* at The National.

"Gielgud said, 'I couldn't decide quite what the chap I was playing was going to look like till I saw someone in the street in sandals, a grown man in sandals. That's it! I had the character, I saw the whole thing. Sandals, I'll wear sandals.'

"And Larry," Constance continued with a glance at me as strong as a laser beam. "Sir Laurence Olivier, Larry. I've never known anyone to extend himself as far as Larry does. He forces his body to do extraordinary things. When he played Othello, he worked until he got his voice down three notes. When he did Coriolanus at Stratford, he had a rock the size of this living room tied to his feet, and when he was thrown over a cliff the chaps backstage gave him a terrible killing blow and he fell down and hung upside down. It was a wonderful effect. Larry would do anything for effect." She chuckled, delightedly, like a child making a discovery. "Of course, he's got a devastating sense of humor, but he's wonderful to work with because he's so generous. And his energy is boundless, absolutely boundless. You can't imagine the extent of Larry's energy. We were rehearsing *Long Day's Journey* when he was involved with all sorts of other things like running the National

Constance Cummings in Arthur Kopit's Wings *(1982), Yale Repertory Theatre, New Haven. Photo: Eugene Cook.*

Theatre besides our full rehearsal and acting the leading role. Incredible."

In Arthur Kopit's *Wings* Constance Cummings created a character of glowing memorability as a woman battling back from a stroke. I was riveted by her ability to assimilate the mannerisms, the pain, the reality of being assailed by voices she could not understand. She was truly remarkable.

At first she was reluctant to play Emily Stilson, the pioneer aviatrix, the wing-walker. She couldn't envision how the play could be made to work on stage. It wasn't a conventional theatre, to say the least. The part demanded that she put together disconnected fragments. She felt it would be difficult, but she accepted. When director John Madden suggested a visit to the Burke Rehabilitation Center in White Plains, she didn't think she could face it. After the experience of observing the patients, she found that the part demanded an avenue different from her usual approach to work. She learned the part the way one masters the multiplication table. She felt, she said, "as if she had lifted the top of her head and was literally spooning the words in."

"Watching human beings fighting to come out of the devastating effects of a stroke gave me a whole new perspective of the play. What had at first seemed to me like going into a bin of loonies became a deep experience." Only once before, Constance pointed out, had she had a deeper input in a role. And that was as Mary Tyrone in O'Neill's *Long Day's Journey into Night,* in which she played a mother addicted to morphine.

"I needed to know what made her the way she was. A friend at the Royal College of Surgeons got me a monograph. I read it, and realized Mary was an adolescent who never grew beyond the emotional age of thirteen."

Her debut performance in *Wings* at the Yale Repertory Theatre was so incisively touching, the play became virtually a one-woman show. She said, "It was difficult to imagine a void, a state of nonbeing. It takes a leap of the imagination to work out what it's like when the brain is only working in little flashes."

When asked why she risked *Wings* at a time when her career was cozy and secure in England, she said, "Every time I do a play it's a risk. You have to be prepared to walk onto the stage naked. There you are, to be looked at and criticized. But you have to take a chance. It's the essence of acting or any art. You have to reach out, to try to express something you really can't express in everyday words—and that's risky territory . . ."

Constance Cummings made the leap of "good leading lady" to "great" so decisively that her performance was hailed by Mel Gussow of the *New York Times* as intensely moving . . . a voyage of discovery; great acting."

"Yes," she said. "How quickly it all goes. It's a long way from Seattle to the Order of the British Empire. How quickly it all goes. But no regrets."

I asked her how she works on a part.

"When I begin to study a part, I record it two or three times on a tape recorder. I get to know what the timing of the other person's speech is, and the timing of my own. Having a tape recorder is like having another person cue you, but only better. No chitchat; your cue keeps coming up and you can play it over and over again at your own pace until you know it."

She continued, "When you start rehearsing, what you do is build and eliminate. You keep refining, purifying, so that you end up doing as little as possible to get an effect. No, that is not like being natural. I think you must present only what relates to the play with a certain amount of discretion."

Talking about the experience of acting delighted Constance and she laughed and said, "Let's talk another ten minutes." She described how she gets out of trouble on stage. "I go slower and slower. It's not very good acting, but I get back in control of myself."

Like most actresses, parts and plays haven't always been there for Constance. She smiled as she recalled the moments sitting at home thinking, "Why doesn't anyone send me a play?" Once, when she found herself talking to opera singer Placido Domingo at a party in New York, she said, "You must be the busiest man to come down the mountain." "Yes," he said, "I am at the top of the mountain." Domingo nodded, "I am at the moment. . . . But it's a terrible business, isn't it? Either everybody wants you or nobody wants you. You can come down from the mountain very quickly." "Ah, well," sighed Constance.

It is difficult to think of Constance Cummings's indescribable iridescence in terms of exact technique, but she repeats her same performance again and again. She has found her own unique way to form a role and can be depended on to strike the same keys night after night. She is a mistress of craft as well as charm. I look forward to many more portraits like her magnificently eccentric gardener, Mrs. St. Maugham, in *The Chalk Garden* which I thrilled to at the Roundabout Theatre in New York, or her ditsy Judith in Noel Coward's *Hay Fever* in London.

As far as I'm concerned, The Golden Girl of the West—or is it The Golden Girl of the West End?—can do no wrong.

Eva Le Gallienne

Whenever I lose a part, can't learn lines, don't know what to do with a scene, whenever I get blue and wonder why I have chosen my frustrating profession, I think of Miss Eva Le Gallienne and I take heart.

On Miss Le Gallienne's eighty-fifth birthday she told a reporter from the *New York Times* that she has no problem learning and remembering lines, and she relishes work whenever an opportunity comes her way. But she regretfully added that "there aren't very many things for old women to play."

Like Peter Pan in her own Civic Repertory's lovely production, she opened the window and took her audience along to Never-Never Land where there isn't such a thing as time. In life as well, the incredible Miss Le Gallienne is ageless.

It was during a dry run of David Susskind's TV production of Thornton Wilder's *The Bridge of San Luis Rey* that Miss Le G, as she is affectionately called by her friends, gave me the courage to continue acting. She had the gnarled hands of a healer, eyes of fjord blue, and a voice as sweet as an angel's.

With limitless empathy she played the Abbess of a convent who lost several of her dearest friends in the bridge disaster, and when she recited the beatitudes, a literary link between the living and the dead, she was unforgettable.

Susskind gave us notes at the 5 P.M. coffee break and informed us that ten minutes had to be cut from the production. Viveca

35 Cents   March, 1

The Theat
Perishin
Says St. John

Don't You
Beliet
Answers the

Eva Le Gallienne in the title rôle of "Pe

Eva Le Gallienne as Peter Pan (1929) on the cover of Theatre Magazine. *By courtesy of the National Repertory Theatre.*

Lindfors's flamboyant actress remained intact, as did Judith Anderson's splendid Marquesa de Montemayor, a masterly portrait of loneliness and selfishness, and so did Hume Cronyn's wily Uncle Pio, but my main scene with Miss Le G as the Marquesa's daughter got the red pencil. Miss Le G made the disappointment seem unimportant, and we made what was left of the scene a moment felt.

Eva Le Gallienne was born in London. Her father, a distinguished poet, essayist, and novelist, was a great literary figure; her Danish mother, a writer and newspaper woman from whom Eva learned Danish and Swedish, enabled her to make her own incisive and unique translations of Ibsen.

Everything about Miss Le Gallienne is theatrical in a way that is not of our fast-paced world. Her voice is inflected with a wide range of rich notes, her ideals are Olympian, her calm can be heroic. Her values and memories are to be cherished. She understood the ways in which one actress learned from older actresses, one generation to another.

In her first book of memoirs, *At 33,* she said that her first meeting with Sarah Bernhardt filled her with such intense joy that it was almost agony. "Sarah Bernhardt put her hand out to me to be kissed. I had been told that she was always treated like royalty. She smiled, bent down, and kissed me on both cheeks. I remember that her teeth had specks of rouge on them from her makeup which was very heavy, and that her eyes were a curious sea green and laughing."

Success came early to Eva Le Gallienne; she became a star when she was very young, at a time when being a star on pre-Depression Broadway was as glamorous as being the Queen of England. Her triumph in Molnar's *Liliom* in 1921 was followed by an even greater triumph in *The Swan* in 1923. The world was hers.

Helen Hayes once told José Ferrer that being in theatre was like climbing a mountain; when you arrive at a pinnacle, you look in the distance at the next peak to climb, and you go way down to the valley so that you can climb to the top again. That was true of Miss Le G's career, but her peaks were more glorious and higher than anyone else's and her valleys not quite so low.

At the very top of the mountain in 1923, she abdicated and founded the Civic Repertory, an experimental theatre enterprise of herculean proportions. It changed the face of American theatre, bringing the repertory system to our shores. From 1926 to 1932,

Eva Le Gallienne in L'Aglian. *By courtesy of the National Repertory Theatre.*

in six seasons and 1,581 performances in thirty-four plays, she achieved her goal, sometimes doing eight different plays in one week.

She produced, directed, and acted in most of them. It was this theatre that dominated the activist theatre throughout the thirties. Courage and imagination became synonymous with her name, her presence on stage and beyond it.

She not only gave reality to the northern women of Ibsen, with whom she had a particular affinity, but also introduced American audiences to their first and enduring look at Chekhov's *Three Sisters, The Sea Gull,* and *The Cherry Orchard,* and the plays of Giraudoux. She felt that the essence of the living theatre and its greatest value for an actor lay in the contact and communication between actor and audience. That was at the heart of her repertory theatre.

She thought of her company as a "library of living plays," making them available to audiences for the presently incredible sum of thirty-five cents to a dollar fifty a ticket. The theatre was always filled, but with the onslaught of the Depression, the subsidy disappeared and she heartbrokenly had to abandon her repertory theatre.

However, she never abandoned her ideals. She felt that the theatre should be like the fine arts, an intrinsic part of our cultural life, always in the hearts and minds of the American public.

The next period of her life was devoted to taking theatre beyond the confines of Broadway. She toured coast to coast in Theatre Guild productions of Rostand's *L'Aiglon,* of *Camille,* and of her very special productions of Ibsen's *The Master Builder* and *Hedda Gabler.*

Miss Le G tells the story about an elderly couple who came backstage in a small Midwest town after a performance of *Hedda Gabler.* They told her that they had driven a hundred miles to be there and they thanked her with tears in their eyes for making it possible for them to see one of the great plays of all time.

Throughout her life Miss Le G has stuck to her principles. She noted when she first arrived on Broadway that "there was plenty of cake in the showcases of Broadway, but the bread was missing." She supplied the "bread"—and what good bread it was!

There are no tricks to her technique; she is totally in charge, at ease on stage. Just sitting in a chair in *The Royal Family* her points were made with logic and by deep commitment to what she was saying. And she has rare vocal equipment; her consonants are more clipped than those of most actors; where five hand movements are used she will use one; with perhaps a flick of the wrist she projects a thought.

Her powers of concentration are immense. She noted in her book about Eleonora Duse that Duse developed a concentration so intense that it could transform a mental image into reality—could make it *felt* and *heard* and *seen*. These were the means by which she "lived her roles"; she actually *became* these women—"she did not force them to become her." The same can be said of Miss Le G.

Critic Percy Hammond said of her in *Rosmersholm:* "Miss Le Gallienne of course is Rebecca West. The words come from her lips as if they were her very own, not a playwright's, so naturally does she utter them. Even in scenes that appear fantastic in their futile and sometimes inexplicable despair, she convinces you of their inevitability."

Simplicity is a quality much sought after by actors and seldom achieved. Eva Le Gallienne seems to achieve her simplicity by an inner stillness, which in turn produces a stillness in her body and face. When she does move, it is most often only with her hands, in one telling gesture. Her vocal abilities are remarkable. Her emphasis of key phrases followed by vivid, changing patterns of inflection and her change in rhythms in subordinate parts of a speech give ever-changing color and variety of meaning to long speeches.

All her technical aspects of acting are effortless; seldom stressed in today's training, they all seem not to create a fancy, embellished portrayal, but serve the life of a human spirit.

Perhaps that was part of her reason for doing *Hamlet,* to explore one of the world's most intricate characters, without the encumbrance of sex. It was a noble attempt to make Hamlet abstract. She brought a new slant to one of the most baffling figures in theatrical literature.

Acting for Miss Le Gallienne is "wiping the slate clean, getting rid of 'me' in order to become the part"; this is the antithesis of the Method, to get oneself, one's personal problems, out of the way; that is the key to her performances. "I work slowly. I cannot leap into a part intellectually. I have to work from the inside out. I have to wait for a part to tell me things, for things to occur."

There are certain actresses who have only to sit on stage and audiences are enthralled. Miss Le G has always been one of them.

Eva Le Gallienne as Queen Elizabeth. By courtesy of the National Repertory Theatre.

She said of Eleonora Duse in *The Mystic in the Theatre,* "The art of acting is the art of communication. To deny this is to deny its reason for existing. Duse may have given the impression of being totally oblivious to the audience's presence, but she was always deeply aware that in the final analysis, it is the business of the actor to convey the content and the meaning of the play. No one could have done this more completely than she did."

The same can be said about Miss Le G. I can almost feel a line, as spoken by her—the throb, the intelligence, the thrust behind it, that inexplicable something, a certain clarity that transforms idiosyncrasies into truth.

Pablo Picasso once said, "You only have yourself, and yourself is a thousand suns in your belly." Eva Le Gallienne has shed the light of her many suns on the American theatre.

Miss Le G has been the recipient of more honors than have been accorded any other woman in the theatre at any other time, but her award of a gold medal from the Society of Arts and Sciences for "virtually affecting our national culture" about says it all. Miss Le G's whole personality is warmed by that elusive light, that glow from within without which there is no such thing as great acting. Miss Le G embodies true creativity, and age cannot wither her a whit.

Jessica Tandy

In the winter sunlight of a high-ceilinged New York living room, Jessica Tandy looked like the person of whom George Bernard Shaw said, "This is the true joy in life, the being used for the purpose recognized by yourself as a mighty one."

Jessica Tandy once called Lady Macbeth a "most womanly woman." The same can be said of this slender actress with the sugarspun white hair. This "womanly woman" has charmed scores of critics with a richness of style that lies in quietness. Jessica's protean professionalism has grown over the decades from capable safety to luminous serenity.

With electric clarity she recounted her earliest memories. She was born in London in 1907, and her life was one of genteel but unremitting poverty. Her voice dipped several octaves only to be caught up in a fluty laugh as she talked about her gritty childhood. "My mother and older brothers, along with millions of other Londoners, waved and shouted at the coronation of George the Fifth. I was left behind, keeping warm with my father in the kitchen, and while he was reading I was amusing myself by crawling into the coal scuttle next to the big iron stove. When my mother came home I was black, covered with coal, and my mother gave my father what for, but I don't remember being punished for it."

Her father, a ship's-rope salesman, died when she was twelve, and her mother worked as a headmistress by day and as a clerk at night. Her mother lived through her children's worldly accomplishments: from the dreary front stoop of a two-chimney brick house, she opened the door to a bright world of literature and theatre. She desperately needed to remove her children from the soot and darkness of lower-middle-class life; this was her driving ambition toward fame.

Every night her mother would religiously read Shakespeare or a chapter from Dickens to her children, and Jessica could hardly wait for her to get to the next scene. "She always put us in the way of worthwhile literature and the theatre. Oh, she was beautiful! I think she would have liked to be an actress herself, but when she grew up, at that time being an actress was truly frowned on."

Jessica made the simple act of recounting her childhood an event, her hands expressively punctuating each remembrance. Her voice rose again into a trill and the most mundane facts took on a glow of importance.

"I was lonely and unhappy as a child, a loner. I didn't really relate to the people around me, but I did have a rich full fantasy life," she said. Her first experiences in the theatre were "magical." She was taken to pantomime and to *Peter Pan*, and identified with Peter. I mean the *real* Peter Pan," she said, "not the Peter Pan that's played in New York. It was a magical, emotionally stirring play which also scared me to death when the pirate had Peter in his toils. When I heard the ticktock of the crocodile my heart was in my mouth. I would go home and stand on a ladder and try to fly. Of course I had some nasty tumbles."

Jessica always knew that she wanted to be an actress. She and her older brothers would put on their own plays. By the time she was ten they had done a "potted version" of Gilbert and Sullivan for Christmas and a *Cyrano de Bergerac* in which she played a Roxanne with "red chilblained" hands.

Jessica and her brothers would go to the theatre for twenty-five cents and sit in the stalls. "We would sit spellbound watching. I remember seeing a Strindberg play and afterward we walked five miles, all the way home, not speaking. Another time, after seeing *The Constant Nymph,* I cried all the way home on top of the public bus. It wasn't just entertainment, it was an experience."

She smiled a wistful smile as she related how a childhood illness frustrated her plans for a scholarship in a good girls' school. In her English class, the other students would complain how dull it was when they read Shakespeare. But having been weaned on

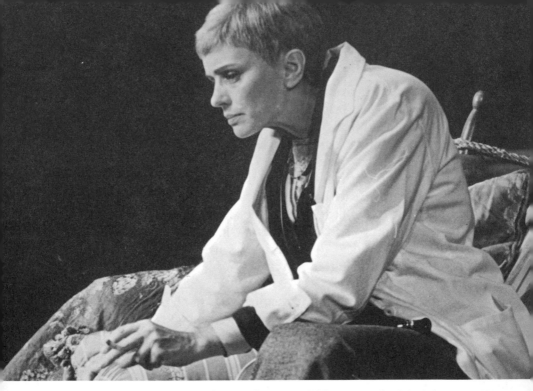

Jessica Tandy as Fraulein Doktor Mathilde von Zahnd in The Physicists *(1964). Courtesy of Jessica Tandy.*

Shakespeare, Jessica found it exciting; even if she didn't understand everything, her mother had laid the foundation. "I learned to respect the punctuation, the words, to love it." Her early knowledge of Shakespeare was the touchstone for her future work.

Given a partial scholarship at thirteen to the Ben Greet Academy, for three years, six days a week, she studied the mysteries of the stage: projection, breath control, the ability to say seven lines at a breath (Sir Tyrone Guthrie's standard requirement).

"A lot of things I learned I later discarded, like using my hands and arms gracefully. One of the professional teachers would point to a paper moon and say, 'First of all, lift your shoulder, lift your elbow, now lift your upper arm, your lower arm, your wrist, then your finger.' I practiced this false movement and got it right and he said, 'Now you're up there, how are you going to get it down?' I said how. 'Drop it?' He said, 'No, no, no, you'll reverse the process. Your finger, your hand, your wrist, lower arm, shoulder.' Well, I had a strong suspicion that he couldn't be right."

During the first couple of years she thought that she'd never make it. She was very ungainly, she claims, her hands very red and awkward, and "I also knew I wasn't pretty and didn't know how to dress." People would write letters or recommendations for her, saying, "Don't bother about how she looks, she's tremendously talented and should be given an opportunity."

Jessica got her first chance in a play called *The Manderson Girls.* After that, she spent a couple of grinding years in repertory companies in Cambridge and Birmingham, where she learned what she didn't want to do. The older character actors would play their parts by the numbers but Jessica would choose a more challenging path. "An awful lot in theatre happens accidentally," she noted. "Sometimes you think, I'm miscast, I don't want to do this part, but the mere fact of doing it, working on it, worrying about it, fussing with it, adds something to you."

Her blueprint for creating a part starts with reading a script as though she is reading a story, as an audience would read it. "Then I go back, if I'm intrigued at all, and read the part again and see what it suggests. I get all kinds of pictures in my mind. It's those constant pictures and memories that evoke things. I find parallels in my life. Then I listen to the other actors. I don't think about it really, it just happens."

Jessica hesitated, "But it's very difficult to explain how you do something." She said that if she has stage fright and her voice goes into the upper register, "I sit in my dressing room and close my eyes. I breathe in six or eight times, hold it for eight, breathe out for eight and do it rhythmically. I find it calms me. I find if you can control your breathing you're more in control of everything."

Jessica started playing the classics as Titania in *Midsummer Night's Dream,* Viola in *Twelfth Night,* and Cordelia in *King Lear* for the Old Vic and the Open Theatre in London, opposite John Gielgud and Laurence Olivier. She played Ophelia in Gielgud's *Hamlet.*

Gielgud would direct by telling her what inflection to make, a technique that is disputed by young actors today; but Jessie glowed with enthusiasm as she talked about it. "It was wonderful. It cuts through a lot of other problems. He also gave me my head. I felt that Ophelia was very much a young woman alone in an absolute man's world. She was a pawn in their games. No wonder she went a little bonkers. When her brother says to her, watch it, kid, and don't go to bed with Hamlet, she accepts it, but when her father says it in such a coarse way, she clams up and can't cope at all."

When we discussed Sir Tyrone Guthrie's production of *Hamlet* in Minnesota, where she played a refined but passionate Gertrude, she felt Ellen Geer's lusty Ophelia of the mad scene was an unfortunate choice on Guthrie's part. Ophelia's grab for the crotch of the soldiers was "too coarse" and she didn't approve at all. It was as if it offended the memories of her mother's values—values of childhood that remained with Jessica and shaped her talent. Her acting might have been too controlled in her youth, but in her middle years it burst forth unexpectedly like a blast of TNT in *A Streetcar Named Desire*.

Jessica Tandy as Blanche Dubois in A Streetcar Named Desire *(1947). Courtesy of Jessica Tandy.*

She came to New York in 1940, where, after three uneasy productions, she was pronounced by the critics as a "fine" new actress. Of her performance in *Yesterday's Magic,* the *Herald Tribune* wrote, "Miss Tandy is perfectly at home in the sympathetic part of the daughter and she plays it with all of her characteristic forthrightness, understanding and charm."

Most of the directors Jessica Tandy worked with had been actors as well as directors. Guthrie, Elia Kazan, Mike Nichols, her husband Hume Cronyn. "They all had some understanding of the acting process so, instead of asking for a result, they would go at it in ways that an actor could understand. They opened the doors for me.

"I'm always amazed when I start rehearsing a play. I go through a long period of time when I haven't found anything, when I feel this is so boring, nothing is falling into place, nothing is happening. Why am I an actress? God, I've got to retire, do something else. I get through that searching stage and I've found a lot of things. Then I start throwing them out. Then: simplify, simplify, simplify. A part is never in place for me until opening night. It takes being gauged by the educated eye of the director, and then two or three weeks in front of the audience. Even after a year of playing a part I find it interesting. I still discover new aspects. And when the play is over I continue to think about it."

She remembered what the director Robin Phillips said to her. "Don't think how are you going to do this; say to yourself, *why* are you going to do this? Then the character decides your action."

Apart from her early years in London, she took little time off from acting except to have her appendix out and to have her children. Through the years Jessica moved through fields of hard work, bringing a high degree of craftsmanship to whatever she did—from parts on Broadway to small mumbles of "Yes, mum, I'm coming," in a spate of Hollywood films like *Forever Amber* and *Dragonwyck,* where she played the gentle English servant with character lines painted on her delicate face. But the turning point came when she married the kinetic actor-director-writer Hume Cronyn, and her contribution moved quickly from the ordinary to the inspired.

Hume rescued her from the relative inactivity of the sound stages and jarred a tendency for noncommittal tentativeness in her acting when he directed her in a one-act play by Tennessee Williams at the Hollywood Actors Laboratory. It was against the studio's wishes that she did *Portrait of a Madonna*. Director Joseph L. Mankiewicz said after seeing it: "I have rarely seen acting to equal hers, even more rarely seen a very tough, invited, professional audience brought cheering to its feet as spontaneously."

Director Elia Kazan and producer Irene Selznick flew out from New York to see it. They were looking for a Blanche DuBois for their upcoming Broadway production of Tennessee Williams's *A Streetcar Named Desire*.

They signed Jessie immediately.

The impulses from childhood that had to do with fantasy, her understanding of genteel pretension, an underlying hysteria, her tranquil desolation and imposing romanticism are phrases that come to mind in defining her Blanche DuBois. She realized completely the defenselessness and defeat of the fallen aristocrat, a ghost from the leisured past who is destroyed by the world's animalism as embodied by Marlon Brando's Stanley Kowalski.

Brooks Atkinson said of her performance in *Streetcar*, "Jessica Tandy has one of the longest, most exacting parts on record. She plays it with an insight as vibrant and pitiless as Mr. Williams' writing."

About the mystery of the rehearsal process, Jessica once said in an interview, "Your author gives you certain lines to say and certain characteristics, and you find as you begin to say these words and think the thoughts of that character, your body will do what that person does. That also relates to the emotional memory bank." Could the lyric martyrdom of Blanche DuBois have drawn on memories of the slums of London? Jessie observed with sweet melancholy that Blanche was a character of many changes, from lyric romanticism to panic and fraudulence, a complex lady with conflicting emotions, several being played out simultaneously. Her Blanche brought to life irrevocably the disorder and the sleaziness of life in the Kowalski apartment in the French Quarter. She gathered to her soul the part of the flawed victim and wore it like a second skin.

Starting with *The Fourposter* in 1951, a two-character play by Jan de Hartog, which opened on Broadway and ran seventy-nine weeks, Jessica and Hume became one of the greatest acting teams in America since the Lunts. The Cronyns have blessed audiences around the country with one entertainment after another, offering their services to Tyrone Guthrie in 1962 when he created "a new

Jessica Tandy as Fonsia Dorsey in The Gin Game *(1977). Courtesy of Jessica Tandy.*

theatre" along the lines of the Old Vic in Minneapolis. Guthrie called Jessica and Hume, "extremely talented, versatile and experienced"; he said "they would offer to both audiences and other actors assurance that standards were likely to be high." And high they were. With excellence of spirit and talent, they played everything from Shakespeare to Arthur Miller to Molière; she was a passionate Gertrude in *Hamlet,* she was a splendidly faded Olga in *The Three Sisters,* who looks with optimism for the secret of life in escape to Moscow; and she played Willy Loman's wife Linda in *Death of a Salesman* with "understanding of middle compassion."

Recently their personal and professional attachment to each other took them to Russia with their extraordinary study of old age in *The Gin Game,* a two-character play so wordy and difficult to learn that during rehearsals Jessica scribbled lines on the table during the gin game. She had fourteen different games going while she was learning the sequence.

The head of the Moscow Art Theatre said of their visit: "They are showing us what the Stanislavsky method is all about."

For the eleventh time together Jessica and Hume played out their private life through their art in *Foxfire,* a play inspired by the simple life of Appalachian farmers in the Blue Ridge Mountains.

Elia Kazan, in writing about them, declared that the most significant factor in their acting is how immaculate the characterizations are. "With Hume Cronyn and Jessica Tandy there is no sloppy, self-indulgent spilling over into their personal life. It's the miracle of great acting. They don't take over the characters; *you* get taken over by the characters."

Jessica Tandy, whose emotion floods through her like sunlight, has, with the technical precision of a surgeon and the honesty of a judge, become one of the nobler ladies of the modern stage.

A serious, plain English girl illuminates a small corner of our theatre with her great light.

Dame Judith Anderson

I t was the twilight of a rainy afternoon in Santa Barbara, California. Keen-eyed and vibrant Dame Judith Anderson waved good-bye to me from the porch of her Tudor house on San Ysidro Lane. We had spent a splendid few hours together and I was full of her words and presence. She looked down at a newly emerging potted plant and said with a wealth of passion, "My black orchid will soon be in bloom. Won't it be lovely?"

In her mid-eighties, one of the foremost actresses of our time seemed to have the immediacy of enduring youth. Australian-born Dame Judith still possesses "star quality," a quality as difficult to describe as the unearthly glow of a distant constellation.

But one quickly begins to understand the will, the sheer force that has guided her so constantly since childhood. Forthright and confident, she always "knew" that she was going to be an actress. "Not only that," she said, "but I knew that I was going to be a *great* actress." She said this with all the confidence of someone secure forever in her place in the starry firmament.

No other member of the Anderson clan had the slightest disposition toward the theatre. Formal schooling was a small part of a happy-go-lucky childhood. A self-confessed "show-off," a "dunce," the black sheep of the family, she would wheel a wheelbarrow with Murray, a collie dog with whom she shared her bed and a weaning cloth soaked in milk. Together they would deliver groceries from her mother's store, do tricks at parties, play hooky from school (sometimes steal flowers), and she would daydream of being a famous actress. All her dolls had actresses' names. "I didn't know about a Duse, but I certainly had a Sarah Bernhardt doll and a Mary Stewart doll. Mary Stewart was an Australian actress. Oh, she was so beautiful," Dame Judith said with her famous familiar signature, a chuckle that starts low in her throat and works its way up the scale to a giggle.

Judith had a natural voice, a rich, mellow contralto, but by the time she was ready to study seriously, her "pale and beautiful father, once a great businessman, a silver king," had gambled every penny away and left her mother with four children and not a cent.

Frankie, or Frances Margaret, as Judith was called then, made temperance speeches and sang "good-bye songs," a common entertainment in provincial Australia, for which she was awarded silver and diamond medals. It was when she heard the extraordinary Melba sing that she knew being on the stage was truly what she wanted to do. "I wanted to be able to do to people what she did, with the same wonder and beauty. People were cleansed and purified by her," Dame Judith said with remembered awe. "I cried tears, I know not whence they came. Tears, the depth of some divine despair." Her elocution teacher asked her: "Why do you say these things?" She replied, "I don't know, but it's all there in the words."

She realized even then that she was only in control when she was acting.

The greater the talent of the actress, the more she needs to find a technique through which to express that talent. Hers was a lifelong journey that began with that childhood realization of her own power. Judith looked twelve years old when she mentioned her youthful mentor, the famed Scottish actor Julius Knight. "I credit him for teaching me stage craft. I went on tour with him playing a repertoire of modern and costume drama."

She had the advantage of running the performance range from ingenues and character parts to leading ladies—invaluable training for a novice. Julius Knight taught her "to stand firmly on her feet, bosom out, and speak up. When you're sitting down you sit with your feet and legs a certain way and you see that your frame is placed properly." That was the beginning.

As a young actress she was always confident, always ambitious, eager to learn the century-old craft of movement and voice control.

Julius Knight taught her the baroque use of her hands by demonstrating that feeling starts from the shoulders and then moves down the arms until it reaches the flexed hand, and always the graceful arc. JK (as he was called) used to stand in the wings and say, "Look at her, look at her, look at Frankie."

As the years passed, with concentration and clarity she would eventually flash into the darkest corners of minds of Lady Macbeth, Queen Gertrude, Clytemnestra, and, of course, her unforgettable Medea. All would be laid bare in her full anguish. Hers is a truly remarkable talent.

Dame Judith learned to make friends with the "beloved enemy, the audience." They were always "the enemy" until you made them your friend. "And oh, they are wonderful when they love you," she said through half-closed eyes, looking like a large cat warming herself by the fire.

The thought of journeying to America was always in the back of her mind, but it took actual shape when she appeared, with an American-Australian cast, in an American play, *Turn to the Right*. An American actor said to her, "You'll never get anywhere in Australia. You'd better go to God's country." She said, "I thought Australia was God's country. Where's God's country?" And the actor said, "America is." She answered, "Oh, Lord, that's an idea," and she immediately sent a wire to her brother: "Tell mother to pack up; we're going to God's country."

Five feet two inches, the spunky Australian girl with the piercing eyes of a sea captain on a whale hunt landed with her mom in San Francisco. How different this wide open, crowded hill town was from staid Australia!

She ran up and down on the docks joyfully singing aloud; she was confident that America would be the place where her greatness would blossom.

Not even a damp reception in Hollywood by the great Cecil B. DeMille dimmed her enthusiasm. He was totally insensitive to her "star quality" and protean skill. He thought her an impossible candidate for films and encouraged her to try her luck in New York. She took his advice, and her eventual triumphal reign on the American stage began with this rejection. It was preceded, however, by a bitter struggle that brought her near starvation, and a bout of flu during the famous killer epidemic.

Dame Judith paused in our interview to give me coffee and

show me her new fluffy black kitten, Captain Buller. She explained, carrying the kitten like a doll, that she always named her cats after Captain Buller, the military hero of the Boer War. Heidi Ho, a smooth-haired dachshund, yapped jealously in the background.

Looking toward a large picture window that framed two cypress trees and a view of the Sierra mountains, she settled herself comfortably on the couch putting a mohair car rug on her lap to guard against the piercing western dampness. With a deep sigh she said, "I've always dreaded interviews. I'm a listener, not a talker—." Dame Judith enthusiastically continued recounting stories of her youth.

Judith Anderson in the title role of Medea *(1947) at the Royal Theatre, New York. Courtesy of the Billy Rose Theatre Collection, New York Public Library at Lincoln Center, Astor, Lenox, and Tilden Collection.*

The energy, spirit, and will that powered the childhood vision of her greatness was always in evidence. She was always ambitious, and aware of the heights she could scale as a performer. She knew her potential, but credited her mother's supportiveness and love for giving her the courage to face a cold new world.

Dame Judith learned early that her strong suit was her voice. It was logical that she would turn a frustrated desire to be a singer into being an actress. She continued to work on her voice and developed a rare instrument of varied melody, pitch, and pace. Her vocal ability was of such richness and evidence that it made theatrical success inevitable.

Her first job as a member of the Fourteenth Street Stock Company in New York was the result of pure serendipity. Still weak from her bout with influenza, she attempted to keep an appointment with an agent. Feeling faint, she went instead next door, to an office that happened to house a stock company. Miraculously she perked up, was interviewed by the personnel there, and was hired on the spot.

Her search for dominance and control was not long in coming. In a season in repertory in Boston, Albany, and Schenectady, doing simple crowd-pleasing plays like *Rebecca of Sunnybrook Farm,* she began to gain the knowledge of how to control her "beloved enemy," the audience.

Her first step toward glory, after working her way up from small parts to leads, came when she drew the attention of William Gillette, who cast her in a good role in *Dear Brutus.* She was on her way. Inspired to change her name, she chose Judith, the heroine in George Bernard Shaw's *Devil's Disciple,* leaving behind forever the image of the scrubby little girl who had wheeled a wheelbarrow on the back roads of Australia.

Her first Broadway role was that of a sinuous siren caught in sinful conduct with Louis Calhern. The picturesque melodrama was called *Cobra.* She was a child of the streets who lured him into sinful rendezvous. A critic said, "Though Miss Anderson lacks the advantages of great beauty, she knows her way among the heated murmurs of sex and represents a most ravishing voluptuary." That serpentine lady was to be the first in an exciting gallery of such ladies to which she brought her imaginative insights, depth, and scope of personality.

Dame Judith never held back her great reservoir of imagination; her rich voice created its own wonderful reality. In an era of theatricality, her progress was meteoric. Drama was larger, louder, and more highly colored than today, and her theatricality was the grandest of all.

After *Cobra* the legendary David Belasco then hired her to star in *The Dove* as Dolores, the senorita who brazenly drove the border boys mad. Judith began to separate her skill from her personality, and to grow as an artist. Again, the critics pulled out their most shining adjectives. "She confirms what one sensed in *Cobra*. This talented young actress will one day possess emotional artistry of the first rank. She shows power hitherto unsuspected, a richness of voice, command of technique, wealth of poise, grace of bearing, intelligence and personal charm that will render her a future career of extraordinary power."

On leaving backstage she walked to her car over petals that had been strewn in her path. The great Charlie Chaplin came backstage and said, "I'll write a play, I'll build a theatre for you. You're wonderful, wonderful, wonderful." That got into the papers, and the next day, when she went to the theatre, front-page headlines covered the city: "CHAPLIN TO WRITE PLAY, BUILD THEATRE FOR JUDITH ANDERSON."

That was wonderful for a moment, but then came a five-page telegram from Belasco addressing her as "This little slut, this pie swinging, so-called comedienne!" And there was more.

She never worked for Belasco again.

It is common for young actresses of Dame Judith's intensity to burn themselves out, but with practical foresight she steered her career straight ahead.

Her Broadway successes continued with *On the Stairs, Crooked Square,* and *Anna.* The turning point came with her replacement of Lynne Fontanne in Eugene O'Neill's *Strange Interlude.* Always confident, secure in the gift of a photographic memory, she said, "I thought I could learn the nine-hour play in two weeks by putting the script under my pillow." It took her *eight* exhaustive weeks of constant boning to conquer Nina Leeds.

And so she began interpreting a series of psychological heavyweight parts. Her acting in Eugene O'Neill's *Mourning Becomes Electra* was called "sharp and malignant and tightly knotted." In *As You Desire Me* by Luigi Pirandello, the review read, "electric, compelling, enthralling, a performance of the grand theatre. Resonant voice, sinuous body, fascinating and expressive face. Complex psychological study of a woman's attempt to adjust herself to people and changing circumstances."

Dame Judith had the amazing flair for making abstractions real through real emotions. She dealt with human profundity and made it understandable and exciting for audiences in O'Neill's gigantic dramas like *Strange Interlude*, in which the characters spoke their subconscious thoughts, and of course in *Mourning Becomes Electra*.

She arrived at her stage truths by private and unorthodox means. Once she shouted her lines against a roaring ocean. When studying a difficult emotional text she would drink enough to get just a little tight, and then let all the maudlin emotion ride itself out. Having taken her feelings to their farthest reaches, she would retain this memory and use the essence of it in rehearsal the next day. She said of a part in creation, "If *she's* there and I know her then *she* possesses me, *she* takes charge."

She had the inflexible will of a great artist who was very selective about the parts she chose to play. Just as there was nothing accidental in her continued success, there was nothing accidental in her approach to a part. By the time she played Lady Macbeth opposite Maurice Evans, the indubitable Judith researched the Lady with the thoroughness of a scientist. During rehearsal she wanted to travel to Johns Hopkins Hospital in Baltimore to study sleepwalking, but an obliging psychiatrist friend conveniently arranged to have a patient in New York hypnotized. Judith was permitted to witness and study the procedure.

"The patient's actions," she said, "were not at all as I imagined them to be. There was no light gliding walk. She put her feet down firmly as though to grip the floor. I noticed that her body was tense and she was all of one piece in her movements. When she was spoken to, she turned not only her head, but her whole body." (Actresses playing Lady Macbeth traditionally walked airily around the room, stopping occasionally to wipe away the blood.) Dame Judith became more and more involved and passionate as she described "the girl, holding her hands that were smeared with lipstick, rigidly rubbing the palm of one hand against the back of the other, away from her body. I decided that I would wipe Duncan's blood off my hands in a similar manner, the smell being in my throat and nostrils as well as on my hands."

Learning lines is totally organic for Dame Judith. "When the *she* in *me* knows all her words, I have the part." Not until she played

Gertrude to John Gielgud's Hamlet did she come to rehearsal with lines learned—she had always waited to learn them in rehearsal in case she wanted to change them; but with Shakespeare she felt it was an entirely different matter. Not content with rhetorical or effulgent vocal conventions, she began to trace her own way, freed by knowing the words. She didn't change a comma.

Her description of the ordeal of opening nights is the classic reaction that most actors feel. "A numbness comes over you in the morning. You begin to perspire through sheer nervousness. You decide to walk instead of taking a cab and you find your walk unsteady. Then you recover slightly and worry that you may be exhausting your energy. And the second night and the third and the fifth can be almost as bad."

Always practical, always ambitious, she worked in movies to support a large family to whom she constantly felt responsible. Starting with a gangster film, *Blood Money*, in which she played the villainess, she appeared with chilling success in *Rebecca, Laura, The Ten Commandments*, and dozens of others. But Dame Judith dismissed filmmaking with a shrug of her shoulders and an impatient tone. "A day's work is exhausting, but there is no sense of accom-

Judith Anderson as Mrs. Danvers in Alfred Hitchcock's Rebecca *(1946)*.

plishment. A scene is shot ten times. You start a picture in the middle or the end. I lose my voice when I work in films because I can't project. Your gestures are limited, and your movements are confined. The camera, the microphone, the machines, and the men in the cutting room—these things have power, they robbed me of the kind of control I want to feel. *They* do all the work. Ugh."

Films are basically a director's and photographer's medium. The frustration of being an object must have been difficult for Dame Judith, since her childhood theme was to be in complete control of herself, the part, and the audience.

Year by year Dame Judith added unique values that are the essence of inspired acting. She illuminated the author's ideas and irradiated the part with inner meanings made visible. The simplicity of her art grew as her powers of projecting abstractions grew. There was a certain inner continuity to her work, a steady technical and artistic development which she maintained against all odds.

Greek tragedy was not the sort of play producers readily brought to the stage. After she starred in Pirandello's *As You Desire Me,* she wanted to play the blood-soaked sorceress in Robinson Jeffers's *Medea,* a Medea who wreaks vengeance on Jason and murders her babies. But even as her triumphs piled high, Greek tragedy was closed to her. Finally, the then young producer Robert Whitehead had the courage to create a *Medea* for her and John Gielgud. Dame Judith gave an electrifying performance, and the record-breaking box office success was justification that Greek classics could be popular.

There is in the back of every actress's mind a pattern, a landscape of dreams. This dream governed all Dame Judith's choices. It began with Eugene O'Neill's *Mourning Becomes Electra,* the Greek legend translated to New England; perhaps it was when she played the daughter that she set her inner landscape on Medea and, later, on Robinson Jeffers's Clytemnestra in *The Tower Beyond Tragedy.* Whatever her inner reasoning, when she played Medea it gave her the instrument on which to use the full octaves of her voice. In addition, she designed costumes with the help of Castille of Elizabeth Arden, and, with pagan nakedness underneath, she was an extraordinary creature of barbarism.

What is it that Judith did to enflame the audiences? Critics said, "The ovations are for the performance of Judith Anderson—a performance that is like nothing so much as a full cavalry charge across an open plain, squarely at the tenuous positions held by the audience. And it is difficult to report clearly. There is a swirl of hooves and sabers, a noise of a million guns, and the positions are taken."

Was Dame Judith's clarity brighter than that of her contemporaries, her music sweeter? One could actually see an event when she acted it. One could always feel the woman's pain and thrill to her personal insights. Audiences were exorcised by *her* agonies. Nightly ovations and Olympian praise were naturally her worldly rewards for her remarkable performances.

Thirty-five years later, when producer Robert Whitehead revived Jeffers's *Medea* for his wife, Zoe Caldwell, Dame Judith was asked to play the nurse. She embraced the supporting part with zeal. Her delight in standing by a young Medea was evident when she spoke of Zoe's unique performance. She called it "remarkable, the best . . ."

Judith's sense of the theatre came from a strong personal ego, always sure, always generous, always truthful. It is within the classic tradition that she found her unique place, her style with depth, strength of feeling, theatricality plus reality. She has always filled her portraits with a passion and vision that seem more than ordinary—always human, but somehow always slightly bigger than life. Because of her unique will, she has taken a heroic place in theatre. She looked deep within herself and found that knowledge about the human condition that is beyond explanation, a communion of knowledge that all artists aspire to reach, and she did.

As we talked, the rain continued to fall and dusk swept in to Santa Barbara quickly.

We went into her living room with its cathedral ceilings, and like a child she showed me her treasures. Her laughter filled the room. Is that her talent, this freedom to delve into dark places? Is that how she makes the grotesque human? Dame Judith was inordinately there, a strong presence, decidedly and definitely there.

Standing alongside her pots of extravagant black orchids she looked like a small child. I left her house and stepped onto the rain-drenched path thinking how much her particular magic and strength had meant to me . . . this tiny pioneer actress from Australia.

Part Four

ASCENDING STARS

Julie Walters

Facing the upper bank of the Thames was a row of impressive looking buildings, the Little theatre at the National Theatre of London. It was five-thirty and raining when I was met at the stage door by a slight-boned girl in baggy gray pants and a black T-shirt that said FOOL FOR LOVE in pink letters. Actors from the afternoon performance of *Wild Honey* were trooping past me to get a breath of air on the embankment as I was signed in.

It was Julie Walters, the Rita of *Educating Rita,* all spunk, flamboyance, and intelligent sensitivity. She was celebrating her success by returning to the stage in the National Theatre production of Sam Shepard's drama of incest and love in the raw American Southwest, *Fool for Love.*

Like many "hot actors," she turned down a number of different kinds of properties to give her vote of confidence to the British system for actors, giving equal time to the stage and screen.

"Oh, God, on the first nights I usually think of the critics. But last night I was fueled with anger; I thought, my friends are out there, it's a small tight theatre, and I will do it for them," she said as she whisked me through the narrow backstage corridors of the National Theatre to the small institutional gray dressing room that she shared with another actress. "I thought, they're going to love the play, and they did. That's the best feeling in the world when things come together that never came together before. It's like doing it together, it's wonderful."

Sitting down on her army cot with her legs tucked beneath her like a curious ten-year-old she continued talking, punctuating her words with self-deprecating chuckles. The telephone rang. "No, I don't see myself as the Virgin Mary," she said, when the casting director asked her to play the Virgin Mary in the National Theatre workshop's Christmas production of the Nativity.

"Tell me about *Educating Rita,*" I asked, knowing we had only half an hour because a line rehearsal had been called a half hour before the night's performance. "Oh, yes, I loved it," she said. "Especially on stage. Being able to talk about the class system, which always made me feel inadequate in life, giving voice to feelings I couldn't give voice to in life . . . oh, awful! When you're with some people it's like they're bloody from another planet. It was wonderful playing those scenes because of the feelings I've always felt and forgotten I felt. It all came dredging out."

The events of her life were like a pile of raw material arranged to satisfy the demands of comedy. *Educating Rita* could very well have been Julie Walters's own story. For if there was grit in the comedy, which there was, it was Julie Walters's *own grit* that gave it this quality. Julie *was* the working-class girl who managed to wage a personal campaign against her dead-end life, her small triumph against ignorance—a familiar Cinderella story.

Delicate and compassionate, she illuminated the grimy conditions of the life of the working class. It was the Cinderella story all over again. But she didn't win her prince, Michael Caine. She won her freedom.

"It all started when I was four or five and I did impersonations of my family, teachers—everyone. I had a feeling of inadequacy, I would do everything through other people; I was always thinking other people had all the answers. You know what I mean?"

Despite her modesty, animation is the most important attribute she brings to the stage; she lights everything on the stage around her. When she "cracks" a part she "releases the character from her soul." She is funny, tender, eloquent, and wise, justifying the current razzle-dazzle of her phenomenal success. Her spontaneity is unique. It's her moment. She's got the star by the tail and is riding bright.

I was struck by Julie's self-effacing honesty and high energy. When she was doing the round of morning shows in America for the movie, nothing was sacred. She sent up everything from being kicked out of the posh Beverly Hills Hotel to ribbing Johnny Carson for his attitude about women. Always wearing blue jeans, she cheerfully endeared herself to millions of Americans, demystifying the snobbishness of English society. She established herself like our Lucy, as a kook, a character.

Her American idols are Karen Black, Diane Keaton, Woody Allen, and Robert De Niro. Like them, her ambivalence about being a star is apparent; unlike them she hasn't remained within the confines of film, but has gone back and forth from the screen to the stage.

She loves being in theatre because it has the immediacy and excitement of life-threatening danger. "There is never the same feeling of danger acting on TV or in the films." On stage, no matter how immaculate a performance, fickle fate can deliver its blow. Julie Walters doesn't mind stopping a play in the middle and making the audience part of a disaster if it occurs. In fact, she's been known to create them.

"I'm sorry, this man is ill. Is there a doctor in the house?" she once asked—a trick she has played to relieve the monotony of a long-running stage production of *Educating Rita*. Walters, the cast,

Julie Walters, Educating Rita *(1983).*

and the audience all share the hysteria, not quite disciplined but fun.

A self-confessed terror in her childhood, she felt that she has inherited a great deal of her spirit from her mother, who never wanted Julie to be an actress; but the passion and drive that were her mother's made her one of Julie's strongest influences. She was always trying to please her mother, who wanted her children to be "competitive, but she only succeeded in making them feel inadequate," Julie said laughingly with a hint of pain behind her voice. "She can upset me more than anybody in the world. Any little thing she says can cut to the quick. The same old scars get inflamed again, you know what I mean?"

"Mother drove all her children around the bend. When one brother got a first-class degree in Cambridge my mother said, 'They're turning them away from Harvard with firsts, My other brother became a priest. Can you imagine?"

When Julie wanted to quit nursing at nineteen and go to acting school she thought her mother was going to kill her. "You'll be in the gutter before you are twenty," her mother screamed—but Julie held firm. "Oh, God, I thought, I've got to get out now or I'll be stuck here and in nursing for the rest of my life."

She feels inadequate about the technical side of her acting. She felt she could do everything without training when she was studying. "I thought, I have a voice, I've got a body, that's everything I need. I never bothered with voice classes, and consequently I have suffered enormously. When I did *Educating Rita,* after a while I lost my voice and had to take six weeks out of the show to learn how to open my throat and how to breathe correctly."

She continued talking about her lack of technique. "I've got no real method. I'm all over the place. When I first read a script I get feelings about bits and pieces; I try to capture the moment of truth. If I can find the moment of truth in the character I believe in the play."

She was particularly interested in the difference between doing *Educating Rita* on film and on the stage. "On stage," she said, "because people can't see your face or your eyes I try to project things with my body. I don't mean mugging, just doing the sort of things that will get the truth over to people at the back of the stalls. When it came to doing the film, God, I had to lose a lot of the character, I had to drop mannerisms because it was as if I was suddenly under a microscope. I felt quite frightened at first, but then I started to relate to the lens and it began to work. But I still prefer an audience. It's more exciting."

Where does all this instant celebrity leave her private life?

She does miss having a steady relationship. The closest she comes to intimacy is her friendship with her "mates," the actors with whom she works. Four years ago, she broke up with an actor with whom she had lived for six years. Now she's on her own and she feels much better. "There are times, though, when I get home from rehearsal and there's no milk in the fridge and there's no this and that, and I think, oh, I just wish there were someone here. You know what I mean," she said wistfully in her cracked-ice voice, and added, "But not very often." What about parts? "Are there any parts you yearn to play?" I said, hoping to cover all the aspects I could in our short interview.

She answered with her usual modest enthusiasm. "When I read this play I said, 'God, I want to do that.' But apart from that, no. It's people; I like to work with people."

The door to the dressing room burst open as her dressing room mate blew into the room with the usual National Theatre actors' energy.

The interview was over.

Whether or not Julie Walters becomes the sex symbol of the eighties as the hyperbole of *Educating Rita* suggested, she will always be a *fine* actress. The real test will be whether she can continue to seesaw between film fame and stage excellence with the ease she is managing now.

She walked me to the stage entrance. As the other actors of the National Theatre began to drift in, she kissed me good-bye as if we had been friends forever and would continue to be so.

Julie's is the gift of contact, the gift of intimacy, the gift of giving.

The Stars of India

Travel halfway around the world to Bombay, a city where the atmosphere is heavy with the smell of oil and musk, and nineteenth-century sailing ships crowd the shining Arabian Sea. The wide streets are gridlocked with bullock carts and sacred cows, and the Raj Arch is lined with one-armed beggars and religious suppliants. This is Bombay, the film center of the eastern half of the world.

This industry is the largest in the world. They make more than eight hundred sixty films a year and have an audience that spans all of Asia, the Middle East, the Soviet Union, England, and the Continent.

A chapter on the stars of India may seem far afield from an account of the great actresses of England or Broadway or Hollywood, but I found a sisterhood there. A straight line goes from the hearts and minds of western actresses to those of South Asia. The Indian and Hindi stars belong to the same heritage as the temple dancers who in ancient times were worshiped as the godhead of life, of sex. It is with the same fervor that today's audiences worship their movie stars.

Until three years ago the buccaneer film industry was as swashbuckling as Hollywood in the heyday of the thirties. Today, as part of the rapidly changing India, it is emerging full-blown into the eighties. TV and the advent of art films have thrown confusion into what was solely a "riverboat gambler" business.

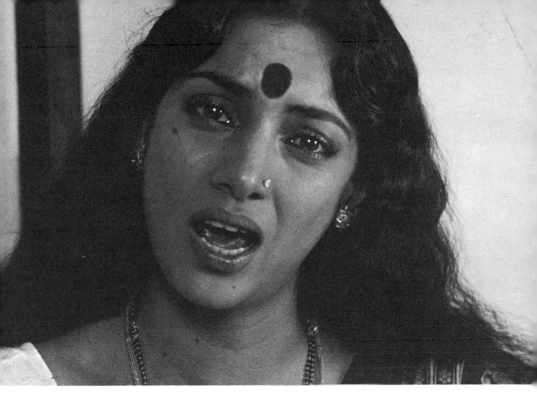

Shabana Azmi as the madame in a brothel in Mandi, *directed by Seyam Bene-gal (1985). Courtesy of Shabana Azmi.*

I spoke with some of the new wave star-goddesses who were trying to change public taste. Shabana Azmi said she disliked doing popular South India films because women were portrayed as sentimental fools who were only around to titillate men. "We have to portray women as men want them, ridiculous, brainless, and seductive. These films are like sugar-coated pills, they put so much sugar on top that toward the end nothing remains."

Sitting in a rose-filled garden, where small green parrots flew from one blazing azalea bush to another, we talked, as actresses do, about technique. The mysterious Shabana was far from brainless. She is a famous actress, the daughter of one of India's leading poet-politicians. She was precise, educated, and very articulate, and an admirer of the Swedish school of film acting.

"I particularly admire Liv Ullmann," she said in a softer-than-feather voice. "Hers is film acting at its most raw and honest."

Shabana was arranging and rearranging a swath of orange cloth around her crisp white Punjabi pants. She looked as if she were a million miles away. It was a little unnerving, as if she stood gazing at a mirage. Suddenly she said, with a passion that belied her calm, "My life is my art, my work. I can't separate them. I'm not the kind of actress who has a watermelon smile. I try to give my portrayals layers of character, even with the typical stereotypes of Indian women."

She continued, "I am willing to play a degraded woman, if by the very degradation of that character I can convey how unfair the system is for women. Yes, woman are changing, and all I want to do is to help our women by portraying them as flesh and blood, real women. . . ."

We talked about her training; it was as exacting as anything that the Royal Academy of Dramatic Art or the Actors Studio provides. She demonstrated one of the eye exercises that she practiced for two years at the National Film Institute of India. Looking at a spot on the wall she said she was taught to stretch her imagination by pretending to look down a well, or two thousand feet into the distance.

I would call that playing the horizon, but to Shabana it was second nature. She seemed to carry infinity in a glance. . . .

On the other hand, beauty-contest winner Poonam Dillon isn't much of an actress. She was described by handsome actor-director Girish Karnad as a "delicious piece of chocolate cake." She earns

Poonan Dillon in popular "wet sari" film (1985). Courtesy of Poonan Dillon.

several million rupees a film and makes more than five or six films a year. Poonam was shooting two films at the time I wanted to interview her, and finally, after a complicated series of maneuvers, I was able to arrange a meeting with her.

Poonam's father, an impressive Sikh gentleman, six foot three and wearing a royal blue turban, answered the door, apologizing for the difficulty I had had in reaching his daughter. Her secretary, sister, mother, and other fixed members of her entourage apologized even more profusely for her absence. "She just woke up and is getting dressed."

Poonam was brushing her long black hair as she came out of a blue and white Hollywood rococo bedroom. Tall and long-legged, with her much-admired bosom pushed up and out, she looked and sounded like a high school cheerleader. She was wearing red spiked-heel shoes and a schoolgirl blouse. She talked about her feelings about being a movie star. Like most of the Indian actresses I'd spoken to, she immediately established that she didn't want to become "a movie star." She had been shy and introverted as a child. But now she loves being a "love goddess," even if it means she has to disguise herself in wigs to escape the persistent attention of the public.

I had an odd feeling of déjà vu as we talked about her "career" and how it felt to be left standing in a wet white sari in the fade-out. I felt like Hedda Hopper talking to Betty Grable in the forties or Marilyn Monroe in the fifties, or like me, Rita Gam, being interviewed about my tight sweater in *The Thief*. The difference was, Poonam liked what she was doing, and had no further ambition than to continue her song-and-dance stories until she got married.

She giggled and offered me a "limca," a lime and soda, after confessing that the innovative obligatory kiss was strange to her and she didn't take it seriously. "I'm a good girl," she said as she bounced back into her Hollywood and Vine boudoir. She took off her red spiked-heel shoes and picked up a teddy bear to punctuate her virginity. There was a pair of black lace panties flung carelessly on the pillow.

Deepti Naval was the third film star I interviewed. She was at the other end of the spectrum. She, too, was a goddess—in the pure sense, a goddess being a woman on a pedestal worshiped by millions. But, like diplomatic Shabana, and unlike Poonan, she was intensely ambitious and passionately articulate.

Wearing blue jeans, she met me at the door of her tiny pent-house apartment that overlooked a wide span of beach and marshlands dotted with camels and laborers. A ten-year-old boy was sweeping the terrace and feeding multicolored birds in cages.

Her apartment was lined with books and posters of Charlie Chaplin and one of Natassia Kinski, nude and hugging the snake in the famous photograph by Richard Avedon. I was surprised to learn that Deepti grew up in New York and returned to Bombay, after some years of emotional upheaval, to become an Indian film star.

Deepti Naval at home, Bombay (1985). Courtesy of Deepti Naval.

Deepti leaned forward confidentially and said, "Many people snigger and wonder why all this harping the same tune of feminism, but the senselessness and absurdity of the South Indian actresses and filmmakers is terrifying." She continued, "Film is a strong medium, and we should use it to spread awareness of our many problems. We have a cause and we can grow."

I asked her about an advertisement in the newspaper for the Society of Protection of Wives. There was a picture of the goddess Sati, who burned herself to death. The quotation under the picture read: "Would you want this to happen to your daughter?"

This barbaric custom is the result of the dowry system, which has encouraged the murder of young wives by the husbands' families when the wives have not been able to come up with the dowry or blackmail. This year alone, four films have tried to deal with this problem of murder by fire, but they have been completely ineffective, particularly in the rural districts.

Today many of these films are examining these real problems of Indian women. Deepti felt that that is what films are all about. She defined her success in terms of what she wishes to accomplish. The women she portrays are women who are changing, flesh and blood, real women in a real world. But she also wants to find a niche for herself in the Western cinema and leave the wet saris to other South Indian sex goddesses.

This chapter on Indian actresses would not be complete without discussing dancers, the *other* goddesses of the Indian acting community. Through them I began to understand the connection between religion, art, and the public's sometimes irrational love for their stars.

It was in a misty dawn among the nine remaining temples of Khajuraho, the ancient ruins in central India, which have for centuries been shrouded in mystery, that I saw the great dancer, one-time film star Protima Bedi, dance.

Sikhs in turbans, ladies in transparent cotton saris, and early-morning tourists from the world over were gathering at the base of the temples. The sun moved quickly to its morning place as if to watch Protima Bedi give a demonstration of the Odissi style of dance. She moved with sensuous control in front of the images of elephants and men and horses locked in sexual embraces. Sacred and profane images of endless imagination, sexy and improbable and wonderful, they had postured for centuries on stone at the base of the main temple. The cool flute and hot drum pierced the morning air with sound.

Protima followed the rules of the ancient movement. The body is held in three graceful curves. Mellow and rounded, she moved as if she were part of the temple, a carved maiden come to life with bells tinkling on her feet. It seemed as if she were moving in and out of the stone.

Her control was that of a Yoga master, and her acting as fine as the finest Stanislavsky-trained performer. She was funny and profound, mischievous and sexy, her hands always moving and her eyes

Protima Bedi in front of a temple at Khajuraho, India (1985). Photo: Rita Gam.

in perfect synchronization. She was an awe-inspiring, hypnotic actress.

She is a great communicator of emotion, projecting thought and feeling through bone and sinew and muscle. Duse would envy the heights of emotional intensity she attained within the confines of the rigidity of the oft-told fairy tales. Wonderfully, she told the stories of her people. They are as varied as the seven hundred million people who live in the vast subcontinent of India.

Elizabeth McGovern and Diane Venora

What book about actresses would be complete without a chapter on young stars, ascending stars? Certainly both Elizabeth McGovern and Diane Venora are just that.

Elizabeth attracted instant media attention in her debut performance of *Ordinary People,* directed by Robert Redford, and Diane for her performance in the title role of *Hamlet* directed by Joe Papp at the Public Theatre.

As young actresses they see farther and probe more deeply than others of their age and experience. They both have the energy and will to give effect to their vision. What they will do with their talent, and how the public, the media, and their contemporaries will feel about them as they grow is in the hands of the gods.

It was during the intermission of a new play at the Public Theatre that I saw a tall, coltish girl with intensely blue eyes leaning against a marble column. She was incredible looking. I thought, if that girl isn't a film actress, she should be.

It was, of course, Elizabeth McGovern, the young actress who was unforgettable as the Floradora girl Evelyn Nesbit in Miloš Forman's turn-of-the-century saga of E.L. Doctorow's book *Ragtime.* As the showgirl with "the face of an angel and the heart of a snake" she lit up the screen with a sense of humor and a wild glint in her eye that were heart-stopping.

What are the stresses born of learning one's art in the bright blaze of publicity? Was she a star created by the high-powered hype of the eighties? How would she handle this delicate once-in-a-lifetime moment? What did she really want to get from her mint-new career?

Only Elizabeth herself can answer these questions. The world rewards beauty such as hers with fame and money and constant attention. Does she want that? Kindness on the lips of strangers and doors opening automatically?

Old friends fall away. Is the bottom line anger and jealousy? How does Elizabeth feel about that? How does she feel about seeing herself blown up to twenty times normal size? How does she react to the world's reaction to her Botticelli-like beauty?

There was a similar moment in my own career when I played the call girl in *The Thief* opposite Ray Milland, and I was practically paralyzed from being taken unawares by the sudden and lethal attention of the public. What had a million dollars' worth of publicity to do with acting? What is the connection between beauty, which one has little to do with, and the craft of acting? Was that a problem for Elizabeth?

I was reminded of the time I was in Manchester, England, doing a taping of *The Time of Your Life* for Jean Dalrymple, when actress Paula Laurence told me that I was like an uncooked egg, round and perfect, unblemished and unbroken. I was infuriated by the comparison. But as the years go by, I appreciate the aptness. The same image could apply to Elizabeth.

There is something of the same untouched perfection about her. Life has not written anything as yet on her face. Her beauty is undefined, her features still unformed, as though she is waiting for life to happen. Her exquisite features are indefinite, her mouth promises to smile more than it does. Only the combination of stubbornness and adaptability in the set of her chin was unmistakable.

We were introduced during the second-act intermission, and I got the feeling that she was wary of anyone's intruding on her private space. I wondered if she was suffering from the familiar malaise of new stars that I call actor's paranoia. I mentioned that I would like to interview her for the book, and when I began making inquiries as to how to get in touch with her I felt as if I were asking for Princess Di's private telephone number in Buckingham Palace.

After many days of detective work, I tracked down her New York agent who gave me the telephone number of Elizabeth's California agent and mentor, Joan Scott, who in turn talked with Elizabeth and told her to call me. After many days of waiting, with telephone answering machines making friends, I finally made contact with Elizabeth, and we made an appointment to meet.

Elizabeth was filled with energy and enthusiasm when she showed up at my apartment on the dot of two, after a singing lesson. She bubbled, "Wonderful lesson, just wonderful." But when I started talking about her career I felt as if I were intruding. I gave her a chicken sandwich and a chapter to read from my book—the chapter about Indian actresses—hoping to break the ice.

Elizabeth McGovern. Photo: Erica Lennard.

She barely touched the chicken sandwich, but she found the chapter on Indian actresses illuminating, and started to melt. She seemed impressed by the independence of the Indian actresses in a male-dominated society, and noted that their creative decisions were independent, as were ours in America.

"Normal as blueberry pie" came to mind when she told me about her midwest background, her U.C.L.A. law-professor father and English high school teacher mother, her graduation from high school in Los Angeles, and agent-mentor Joan Scott's discovery of her at a school play.

She lived through a stimulating and frightening time when she went to Julliard. There was a lot of pressure on her when, as a first-year drama student, she was cast as the girl next door in *Ordinary People*.

"Adulation comes to you in strange ways," she said in a wondering tone, "I got such a disproportionate amount of praise for doing *Ordinary People* that when I went back to high school and walked down the corridors I was pulled in every direction. I didn't really have time to develop. I found that I got everybody's attention, but that in reality nobody could deal with me."

She takes herself seriously as only the young can do. From my point of view as an actress, I felt she would steer clear of the dangerous waters that can drown "a beauty."

The year Maureen Stapleton won the Academy Award for *Reds,* Elizabeth won a nomination for *Ragtime*. Elizabeth had researched the part meticulously. Now, without a note of tentativeness she said, "Acting makes me feel alive. I particularly love exploring a script, and when I play, I love looking into someone else's eyes. It's just a great and wonderful feeling you get when you are in the middle of doing it."

Elizabeth wants to commute between stage and film, and does just that. In quick succession she made a comedy with Dudley Moore called *Lovesick,* and the charming *Racing with the Moon,* right after *Ordinary People* and *Ragtime*. Then she went to Alaska to do George Bernard Shaw's *Major Barbara*.

She became a Joe Papp favorite and began working regularly at the Public Theater. She played the daughter in *Painting Churches* by Tina Howe. This is rapidly becoming a classic. She appeared in *My Sister in the House,* and in David Hare's intellectually satisfying *Map of the World*.

When does the pre-adolescent's dream of being a veterinarian, a painter, and a ballet dancer give way to the dream of being an actress? Some time during high school, Elizabeth spent the summer in San Francisco's American Conservatory Theatre and found theatre stimulating. It made her feel as if she was doing something useful. That initial passion has remained and has grown. She once said in an interview, "When it works and I can do it well, I feel as if it's a good thing to do for people. When I see a good play and my imagination is stimulated it just makes the sky wider."

Her philosophy is that of an actress for all seasons. "There must be actors and actresses who definitely must want to win awards, but I'm not one of them. That's not where the real joy is." With several movie triumphs and with one year of formal training, she worries more about her technique than where her career is going. Elizabeth thinks of herself as a "bread and butter actress" who will go anywhere the work is. When asked by a friend if she was ambitious, she said, "Well, compared to Joan Crawford, I'm a sweet little cream puff."

I think Elizabeth is an actress whose work will get more interesting as she gets older. Technique and talent will shape her career. Elizabeth said that she is never satisfied with her performances. "It is a constant source of frustration, but there is joy in the frustration. What's perfect, anyway?" She continued, "I don't believe in art as torture. Art is fun. I think it's a celebration, even when it's dealing with the dark side of things. The act of sharing something is a good feeling."

If good luck is opportunity plus readiness, I believe Elizabeth McGovern has that and will be a part of our film and theatre world for years to come. I think there is little chance of her becoming a repertory nun, dragging a little red trunk from regional theatre to regional theatre. Her indefatigable curiosity, her levelheadedness, and shimmering beauty will take her far; and if I may add a fleeting observation, for luck, in the bright light of my New York apartment there was in her profile more than a little resemblance to a young Eva Le Gallienne.

Diane Venora was the exact opposite of Elizabeth McGovern. Diane reminds me of Maureen Stapleton, except that she is young and tall and her body willowy. Diane has luminosity, intensity, but she is funny, too. Waves of warmth come from her, and you feel that hers is a talent of rampant individualism.

My meeting with Diane was as spontaneous as saying hello to my own children. We hugged each other on being introduced to each other by talented Larry Sacharow, the director of *The Sea Gull,* in which I played her mother Paulina.

The Sea Gull opened a Woodstock after four weeks of rehearsal to audiences whose appreciation was absolute. The play is about love, and Diane Venora's understanding of the play's super-objective was marvelous.

I interviewed her in her little studio in the woods of Woodstock to find out how she built her extraordinary characterization of Masha. One wall in the studio was completely covered with pictures of Russia, and charts of different emotions. There were color reproductions of painter Isaac Levitan's storm, haystacks, woman walking among the birches, and a winter's day.

These pictures of Chekhov's painter friend captured the awesome nature and the same human fragility of Chekhov's plays. Diane laughed and said, "The acting process is so chaotic that pictures and words tell me what to do. I discover where I have to go from act to act, and what it is going to cost me emotionally to get from one scene to another. Acting is like birthing a baby."

Diane works from her imagination. Sometimes an actor's imagination is a more powerful tool than reality for her. Her method is infallibly inspiring for her. She tacks onto a wall things that stimulate her imagination, and finds the inner development through these pictures.

Her father was an amateur photographer, and consequently the visual automatically became part of her creative tool kit.

"One night," she said, "I went to the barn in the woods. It was late. It was rainy, a dark, haunting place, and suddenly the ambience of the fourth act became clear as I heard the rain hitting the roof."

But the real breakthrough occurred for Diane's Masha when she lost the cap of one of her front teeth and was left with a black and gaping hole when she smiled. In her physical and mental pain she became five years old. I quipped, "An actor will go to any length to find the character." But when I said, "I feel so badly for you, Mashenka," on stage, everything was full, was really there. . . .

Fortunately the tooth was replaced on her day off. Since she has to go on to other parts, a gaping hole was not an asset. But the accident had already contributed a certain vulnerability to the character of Masha, and the pain she had experienced she kept and added to her believability on stage.

After dropping out of the Boston Conservatory of Music, she went to Julliard "to get the best training I could find." Today, because of that training, she has one of the strongest and most interesting voices in the theatre. Crediting Robert Williams with teaching her everything about speech she said, "Consonants are like cut glass," and yet, when she began, her teachers told her that she was a "piccolo trying to be a tuba."

Although Diane's looks and essence reminded me of Kate, my own daughter, even to the slant of her eyes, it didn't make acting with her the least bit easier. The resemblance haunted me, but the stream of emotion that I hoped would become a river didn't happen right away. During rehearsal Diane was self-indulgent; she ranted and agonized as she created Masha, while I prayed. I tried to find my emotional truth in the wee hours before I fell asleep. Diane hunted hers in public.

At best, rehearsals are an intensely personal time. After many hours, fueled by cups of coffee and conflicts, our Chekhovian ladies began to live.

For three weeks through good rehearsals and bad, we wandered around trying on the emotional truths of one another. It was a time for finding things about one's life in order to nourish the work.

Diane and I had different approaches to the journey toward the center of our characters, but slowly, despite the difference in our training, we found the true life force of our coexistence on stage.

Our first run-through with an audience was a shock, and despite the excitement and electricity that a live audience provides, our timing was just a beat behind, and at a crucial moment when we were supposed to be listening to a violin play and it wasn't there, Diane hummed and I improvised my line, pulling the scene out of the fire. I realized that our minds were meshing, and the magical stage connection was taking place.

Diane began the craft of acting later than many of her peers. She was from Hartford, Connecticut. Her mother was English and

Diane Venora as Hamlet *at the Public Theatre (1982). Photo: Martha Swope.*

her father Italian, the blessing of which combination is evident in her delicate good looks.

"Acting is about courage and truth. You have to use your heart and your soul to act." said Diane. "Without it, it doesn't fly."

It was New York's showman Joe Papp who discovered Diane when she was playing a high-tech Hippolyta in *A Midsummer Night's Dream*. He thought she looked like an exquisite boy, all verve and in black, and he asked her to read for a play that he had Kevin Kline in mind for, but he had always wanted to produce it with a girl. Diane calls it her "life break."

Papp said he had wanted to do the play for years, and when she asked what the name was and he said, *"Hamlet,"* she was so stunned and nervous that she asked, "Who wrote it?" With a straight face he answered, "Shakespeare."

Hamlet, as played by a woman, has traditionally been played by a star of great stature. It is one of the parts that has always been savored as the crowning achievement of a lifetime. Sarah Bernhardt played the Danish prince with the additional burden of having only one leg. Eva Le Gallienne and Judith Anderson were in full faculty when they played Hamlet, but the critics were less than generous in their appraisal of them. Papp's desire to do *Hamlet* with Diane was rooted as much in timeworn tradition as in enterprise.

And what a tortured Prince of Denmark she was; there was a wide range of critical acclaim and opinion, but the consensus was that Diane Venora was a wonderful young actress, a talent to be welcomed and encouraged.

"I felt like Pygmalion," said Diane at a benefit dinner. "To be loved by Joe, to have that privilege to play that part with Joe directing. Things happen at the right time. Your energy and soul create them!" She quipped, "Mr. Papp, now that you've made a man of me, what am I fit for?"

Her credits grew quickly and now include: Francis Ford Coppola's *Cotton Club,* Bob Fosse's *All That Jazz,* and the miniseries, "A.D." and "F/X." Diane is equipping herself to make films and to act on the stage with equal ease.

There is a wildness about Diane, an inability to accept things as they are, combined with an evangelistic sincerity. Between scenes backstage she didn't indulge in actor banter, or small talk; she listened to Mahler on her Walkman and studied a bible on healing sickness. All her energies were preserved for the moments on stage. Even when her three-year-old daughter came backstage, she couldn't hear her when the child asked if mommy was really crying on stage.

Like many actresses, Diane has mementos of her inner life sitting on her small dressing table—pictures of her child, a postcard of Garbo and Marlon Brando; and written with a lipstick pencil on the mirror are the words: "Dare, Courage, Hope, Faith."

Will Diane Venora be the Vanessa Redgrave or Jane Fonda of the eighties? Given the exposure and the opportunity, I feel Diane could lend herself to "legend." Time will tell. . . . In the meantime,

I look forward to seeing her many revelations of the human heart.

Her voice softening to a whisper, Diane said, "It's almost like belonging to a religious order to be an actress. Acting is spiritual belief. You go out and gather your material, then you bring it back. Like a nun in your cell you pray, and meditate, and work it out, and then you give yourself to the public. You fight and revolutionize the world through great plays. You have to protect your instrument and your body, but sometimes you have a lapse of faith; and you must give all yourself back to an audience, your heart, your soul, your knowledge."

She paused for a moment and said, "Rita, would you like a glass of champagne?"

Afterword

ctresses learn from one another and pass on something of themselves and what they have learned from generation to generation. I hope this book has contributed to this process.

Julie Harris once told me a story that illustrates this tradition that spans generations and illuminates theatre along the way. I would like to pass it on to you.

On one of Sarah Bernhardt's numerous American tours she bestowed upon a young American actress her very own "strawberry" handkerchief that she lost as Desdemona in *Othello*. As a token of her affection it became a badge of honor, a talisman to be passed along from decade to decade, whenever another exciting young actress came along.

On the occasion of the Broadway opening of John Van Druten's *I Am a Camera*, Helen Hayes presented the symbolic memento to Julie Harris. She in turn gave it to Susan Strasberg on the opening night of *The Diary of Anne Frank*, with the admonishment to pass it along when she found an actress worthy of the gift.

Julie told me that she thought Susan still has the handkerchief.

I hope that *Actress to Actress* has answered some of your questions and has given you insight into the lives of these great and generous ladies. Mostly I hope that I have caught not only a little of their elusive spirit but also that of many of the wonderful actresses I haven't mentioned because of the constraints of space. I hope they too will remain in your thoughts. When you see them you will see the light, the magnificent light that radiates from each one of them.